KEEP WINNING KEEP GOING

USE PERSEVERANCE TO WIN LIFE

Gautam Sharma

I0843256

(Dedicated to valued readers)

COPYRIGHT

Table of Contents

INTRODUCTION

This book will help you use perseverance to win life. Being successful, winning life and being happy can be learnt as a straightforward path: firstly define your goals keeping in mind their purpose and defining the resources that can be utilized, set your full focus/intentions to achieve them, maintain total optimism and enthusiasm in your activities. Use creativity and dedicated effort and keep acknowledging your accomplishments,USE PERSEVERANCE TO WIN LIFE.STEPWISE: FIRST DEFINE YOUR GOAL/GOALS KEEPING IN MIND THE FINAL PURPOSE AND RESOURCES NEEDED, SET YOUR FULLFOCUS/INTENTIONS TO ACHIEVE THEM AND MAINTAIN FULL OPTIMISM IN YOUR ACTIVITIES.USE CREATIVITY AND DEDICATED EFFORT AND KEEP ACKNOWLEDGING YOUR ACCOMPLISHMENTS.MAKE SURE OF KEEPING YOUR MIND, BODY, SPIRIT AND EMOTIONS IN HARMONY AS YOU VISUALIZE YOUR GOALS BEING ALREADY ACCOMPLISHED.WIN LIFE, ACHIEVE WHAT YOU WANT ANDREMAINHAPPY.C.arify your goal. Base it on your purpose, needs, and abilities. ...
Intend to achieve your goal. ...
Maintain optimism. ...

Live in the present. ...
Acknowledge your accomplishments. ...
Try new experiences. ...
Care for you mind, body, emotions, and spirit.Visualize your goals achieved already.

Would you like to get what you want in life every time? Become more happy long term, be more youthful with a healthy body, keep joyous relationships,have satisfying work and income, enjoy big houses, cars, and vacations? Ever wondered how so many people are successful and some lead extraordinary lives-as far as improving civilization and changing countries? Think for a moment about the greatest people over history. There is a distinct, common attribute that has made many men and women extremely successful and renowned over centuries and across continents. From Alexander the Great(356 BC) to Cleopatra, Genghis Khan, Michael Angelo, Joan of Arc, Mahatma Gandhi, Winston Churchill, Marie Curie, Einstein, Thomas Edison, Benjamin

Franklin to present day outstanding people as Bill Gates, Warren Buffet, some other billionaires and world leaders. It's just not mental or physical prowess, talents, education, training or good luck that worked for them. The outstanding common attribute among all successful and extraordinary people of excellence across all space and time has been the quality of perseverance, attitude, and motivation.

It's been about keeping on going towards their goals in the face of denials, obstacles, failures, and opposition. The unstoppable keep on going; whatever the odds, slowdowns or roadblocks and they achieve success, victory, and fame. This book will help you gain the magic of perseverance, motivation and determined attitude. You can also become very persistent and super successful. Let us look at what it is and why it is so important. Perseverance is the attitude and the personality trait to continue with determination on a set course of action to overcome difficulties, failures or opposition until the required goals are achieved. There are several reasons why perseverance is important:

1. 1. It shows that you are ambitious and that you have high goals and objectives to achieve. If you want to go places, you will have reason to find ways to reach there.

2. 2.Your ambition and subsequent drive make you stand out and make others notice your determined, determined personality.Others are drawn to your positivity.

3. 3Perseverance makes you garner skills, experiences, and abilities. The process of working harder to overcome failure helps you acquire new, peripheral skills or hone onto the current ones.

4. Working   harder   helps   build   inner

strength and stamina. The determination to think and work is to keep going on doing activities methodically and consistently going step by step doing activities that are required for your goals. Reasons Why perseverance is the Key to Success?

In simple words, perseverance means the attitude and personality trait of working hard and trying again and again until complete success is achieved. Here is why perseverance is the key to success and why you should develop it as a vital personality trait.

1. perseverance makes you an expert

You may not be good at doing something for the first time but you will get better at it when you keep trying for the second time, third time and so on. With perseverance, you will continue to do the same thing over and over again until you achieve complete success. This will make you an expert in whatever task you are doing.

2. Being perseverant will motivate you to try

harder. Being perseverant means you will keep trying again and again. With every attempt, you will inch closer to success. It will motivate you to put more effort to get closer to your goals when you see that there is an actual difference between where you stand right now, and your previous effort. Self-motivation is an important aspect of being successful.

3. perseverance is a sign of being ambitious.

Only those people who are highly ambitious can incorporate perseverance into every aspect, every little thing that they do in their daily lives. When you keep attempting something with perseverance, everyone around you will look at you as an ambitious person. It will build a positive personality image for you, a key in shaping the outlook of a successful persona.

4. perseverance will set a good example to your associates and peers.

A reason why perseverance is the key to success especially in workplaces is the reason your colleagues and subordinates will be inspired by your level of perseverance. When they see you achieving your goals with determined perseverance, they too will try to imitate this trait. This will result in an overall boost in productivity and efficiency for your team, making perseverance a highly regarded personality trait in any workplace.

5. perseverance teaches you the value of success

Are you under the false notion that success can be achieved easily by manipulative tactics? Do you think that success can be easily bought? Do you think that success comes with just a little bit of effort? If you have these untrue thoughts in your head, perseverance will teach you that success is not that easy to achieve. As you keep attempting to achieve a goal over and over again, you will understand the true value of success. It will enlighten you about the amount of hard work and dedication required to make something happen, preparing you to give your best shot at everything in life if you want to be successful.

6. perseverance will help you gain experience

Being perseverant means getting up after a failure, learning from your mistakes and trying again. This whole process will help you gain experience, which is vital if you want all-rounded success. The Multiple numbers of attempts at the same thing will help you find out the things that can go wrong, the things that are crucial to a process or the things that are not required at all. This experience, which was a result of perseverance, will teach you stuff that books and procedure manuals don't.

7. perseverance will make you aware of your weakness

To be successful, you need to be aware of your weaknesses and your faults. Your weaknesses will only be exposed when you analyze your failures and try to find out the things you lack to accomplish something. This is only possible if you are mentally prepared to accept failure, try again, fail again and keep trying until you iron out all your weaknesses to finally succeed. This is why being perseverance is the key to success.

The most effective words for a lifetime of achievement, success, fun, happiness, joy, and fulfillment: "Keep going. Keep going towards the light, your goals, towards the promise of so much goodness that awaits you. With joyous feelings, hope in your heart, and a song on your lips keep going and receiving achievements, success, love, friendships, fame, fortunes and all else you had imagined. See the pure white light beckoning you, find your path through whatever comes in the way and keep going.

perseverance-The State of Mind

Success is something we all wish for, isn't it? Undeniably, those who attain great things are those who don't know when to give up. Whether you wish to achieve something or want to lose a few pounds or any goal that you are willing to succeed in, you need to be strong and persistent Indeed the most successful people in the world have the key quality of perseverance which makes them assume impossible actions to be possible. How many of you can claim with confidence that you have applied perseverance and consistency in your everyday life with some measure of success? I think the majority of us dream of incredible things but just lack perseverance or the willpower, to follow through to accomplishment. People give up too soon as they have the wrong expectations of themselves and the results. They expect the mode to be easy, and they are amazed when they find the reality to be contradictory. Their enthusiasm quickly melts and they quit. What does being willpower and perseverance mean? It is a cliche to simply say "don't give up".

One of the best illustrations perseverance is the state of mind and sustained effort necessary to induce faith. In other words, it exemplifies that determination mixed with perseverance backed by the desire makes a strong tool to ensure the achievement of the goals". The meaning of the term perseverance is the quality that allows an individual to continue doing things even if it is tricky or opposed by other people. This is not something someone does with external goals; however, it is something someone does internally. Perhaps we all are aware of the fact that in the face of pain, anguish, suffering, and defeat; it may not be easy to stay persistent. In simple words, perseverance means the personality and attitude trait of working harder and harder and trying again and again until success is achieved. Abraham Lincoln is a leading example of perseverance and strong willpower in action. Known as one of the renowned presidents in history, Abraham lost 8 elections before he, in the end, became president. He also lost his fortune when he starts losing his business twice and could have chalked himself up to being a loser, but he didn't. However, he didn't lack his determination and believed he could achieve his dreams. If you are passionate about something, chances are you're determined to move towards that activity or thing. It is the quality that motivates people to do things however difficult or unpopular they may be.

Chapter One

Keep going until you are successful

The conventional definition of perseverance is: "not letting go or refusing to give up; persevering perseverantly; firm or obstinate perseverance in a course of action despite trouble." It is a developed state of mind much like grit. It is the trademark of achievements since perseverant persons push through difficulty, anguish, and pain which refers to the setbacks and roadblocks when pursuing an objective. As the significant component of self-discipline, determination and perseverance also provide its own inspiration and motivation. You become more enthusiastic to do something incredibly when your activities started showing results. For instance, when you want to lose all those extra pounds and start exercise and to workout, you will be more enthused when you lost 20-25 lbs and your present wardrobe starts fitting loose perseverance can conquer almost any challenge. When you turn your mind to something and are eager to do everything it takes, by putting in the time and adjusting your plan to get there, you will eventually know the supremacy and power of determination. Some of the major factors or symptoms of lack of perseverance are indecision, not being clear in what you want, lack of proper planning, weak desire, fear of criticism, feeling of insignificance and lack of going all out. You may not be fine at doing something for the first time but you will get better and better at it when you keep trying and believe in yourself for the second time, third time and so on. With perseverance and consistency, you will continue to do the similar thing over and over again until you accomplish complete success. This will make you a proficient in whatever job you are doing. You have to believe that your victory is guaranteed and no obstacle will stand your way.

Billionaires and political leaders had failed several times and have thought of giving up college but they finally come out ahead as big winners. Edison also made more than 10 thousand experiments before he accomplishes something in making the first talking machine.

As the primary factor of self-discipline, perseverance also provides its own motivation. You become enthusiastic to do something when your actions started showing great performance and results. Courageous perseverance is the main factor than any other that can promise success. And success is somewhat we all want, isn't it? But to be victorious takes perseverance. Whether you want to lose your extra fat, get an A in a class, or any goal that you want to succeed in, you need to be perseverant. It is the difference between a successful result and a failed one due to giving up.

Perseverance has other names — determination, perseverance, a can-do attitude. When getting starting on your vision for success, first and foremost you need to identify your desires and wants. It is when you know the way; you can get a source for inspiration and keep yourself encouraged next, figure out how to achieve what you want? This makes it easier to attain it. Make your objectives actionable every day and follow through. All your objective-setting and planning will go to waste if you won't be able to build up discipline and good habits. Be positive in your work that you will attain what you want. Perseverance separates the losers from the winners. Those who persevere understand that luck is something only failures believe in. Success in life depends on your motivation to never give up, even when the reward is delayed.

How to stay perseverant?

Like all states of mind, perseverance is based upon specific causes. Take a piece of paper and write down a life goal, what you desire, and answer the questions; what is your definite purpose. Knowing what one longing for is the former and, perhaps, the most important step toward the growth of perseverance. Strong motive forces can easily overcome many hurdles of our life. Similar questions like why do you want to accomplish this goal? How will it profit you and the more essential, how will it benefit others? In order to survive your purpose, you have to keep the focus on why you want this purpose/ goal or what the positive results will be in your life? We do have to keep in our mind that our purpose in this world is also to add value to others. If your wishes focus on your own gratification you will sooner or later fail or die a lonely miserable life.

All successful people who have attained great things in their life did so through both willpower and perseverance. Even when they failed, they got encouragement and kept going. But we all know that staying determined and perseverant is difficult. In any conversation of the qualities of the most successful people, it is always declared that perseverance is one of the, most significant factors in success. Major success rarely comes easily or without an enormous deal of attempt. Often the only distinction between those who succeed and those who do not is the capacity to keep going long after the break has dropped out. It is comparatively easy to persist when things are going smoothly and we see progress, however, great perseverant people have found several means to keep going in spite of major setbacks and a lack of confirmation that they are driving near toward their goals.

Some of the significant things that perseverant people have in common that keep them moving on long after so many people have given up:

Visualization for success

perseverant people have a vision or goal in mind that encourages and drives them. They are often visionaries and dreamers who see their lives as having a high purpose than simply just spending their life. Their vision is deeply entrenched, and they concentrate on it continuously and with great energy and the state of mind. They often think of this dream first thing when they wake up and the last thing prior to they go to bed. Accomplishing this goal becomes the crucial and focal point of their life and they dedicate a major portion of their time and energies towards attaining it.

- **Unshakable self-confidence, self-belief**

Those persons who defeat the hurdles and accomplish greatly are often illustrated as "marching to the beat of their own drummer." perseverance people know what they wish for and are seldom swayed by the view of the masses. To have the perfect intelligence of who they really are, allows the perseverant to carry on without being seriously affected by what others think of them or, being appreciated, or being understood by those around them. At the same time as that inner confidence gets shaken, but never gets shattered and continuously acts as a source of courage and strength.

- **Inherent passion to succeed**

There are so many inspiring Entrepreneur and Industrialists who always speak, "If you really desire to do something, you will surely discover a way. If you do not, you will find an excuse." perseverant people never look for any excuse. What keeps perseverant people going is their potent level of desire. Repeated failures, losing periods and dead ends, when it seems like no progress is being made, often come before some breakthroughs happen. perseverant people with high will-power have the intensity, state of mind, and inner energy to keep them motivated and going through these hard-hitting times.

• Talent to Adjust and Acclimatize

perseverant people have the capacity to acclimatize and adapt their action plan. They do not stubbornly persevere in the face of indication that their plan is not running but look for enhanced ways that will increase their probability of success. The motivated and perseverant see their life journey as a bunch of dead ends, adjustments, and deviations, but have total faith they will reach their final objective. They are not attached to their ego and are rapidly willing to admit when something is not working. In addition, they are fast to adopt the fresh ideas of others that have been shown to work well.

• Key success habits

As someone truly said, "Motivation is what gets you going ahead. Habit is what keeps you going."Highly perseverant people know it is very tricky to stay constantly motivated, chiefly during hard and the most difficult times and when it appears that no development is being made. They have come to rely upon their self-developing and discipline habits they can count on to carry on the path toward their ultimate goals. They believe the results of the hard work they make today may not be seen for a longer time, but they strongly believe that every single thing they do will count toward their end results.

- **Commitment to acquire new skills**

perseverant people understand the worth of any objective and reaching will take attempt, time, and constantly learning new skills and thoughts patterns. They welcome fresh ideas and change and continue searching for means they can incorporate these into their lives. Ongoing learning is seen as part of a continuous process through which the highly perseverant continually expand the range of tools that they have to work with. Naturally curious type persons not only see learning as a way to reach their objectives more quickly, but they also see self-learning as a way of life. Learning and constant growth do not end at a certain age or phase of life, but they are the spirit of life itself, and thus never-ending.

- **Role models as mentors and motivators**

While it may come into sight that highly perseverant people act without help and don't require any person, most have carefully chosen peoples they follow and admire. These can be individuals who are truly involved in their lives as guides or they can be figures who they have read about and who have extremely impacted them. Such people are often misunderstood on the grounds that they can make those around them feel uncomfortable. The ingrained models assist motivated persons to maintain and motivate themselves in an atmosphere that is not always kind and supportive.

The winners' circle defines perseverance as refusing to give up when faced with opposition or hardship. It could be expressed as simply as trying again and again until you keep scoring at sports, maintaining relationships or succeeding at work or businesses. The greatness that you have, the greatness of the condition, is not calculated by what is accomplished. It is calculated exactly by how many times you pick yourself up and try to accomplish something. Among all of the values and morals we can have, it seems perseverance is the consistent element in most people who thrive and succeed, no matter what they are succeeding at. We all seem to understand or know that all popular personalities have perseverance in huge quantities. They have to keep their mind strong, keeping the boundaries of patience in order to attain the new records. Yet, you can see perseverance all over the place you look, even for the job you get paid to do, so there ought to be something incredible to it. If in case you are evaluating what amount of struggle it would take to give your career a boost up, you might come across in the direction of your own perseverance. You need to be clear about what you are determined to achieve. What is the result you are in the hunt for? If you need to gather knowledge or resources, then go get them. Once you have your objective, your plan, and the resources, then goes after it with dedication and enthusiasm. Stay focused every day until you get the outcomes you defined. It is also OK to occasionally get propped up by close relatives, family or friends to keep the required attitude that comes with perseverance. perseverance is not about the trouble-free road, even though few people make attaining success look easy. perseverance is about systematic and continued to do something even when there is a good reason to give up. perseverance is about the basic confidence of knowing your vision is the right thing to pursue.

Make perseverance a lifelong habit

Another most significant piece to having the higher perseverance level is having support. Sometimes when it came to the list of things we wanted to accomplish personally, having a team of people who were above or on your level made you want to persevere and keep going for your aspirations. It is healthy and nice to have a supportive team like family, close friends, relatives, religion and particularly mentors that can be there beside you when you necessitate an additional boost up of motivation. Support from others is always advantageous, but not always simple to find. If you feel like you don't have a mentor or guide in your support team that you could, in fact, talk and sit down to about your aspirations, make an effort to find one, particularly one that has been where you are and who is at present where you are aspiring to go. There is no sense in having a support team that cannot bond and connect to your goals for the reason that they do not have any aspiring goals themselves. You need to evaluate your crowd cautiously and warily. Having a good imagination and thoughts also helps when it comes to perseverance. When you can visualize and think about your "dream future" no matter what that might be, these visions every so often can get you through the harsh days. Do not let one failure in your journey of life to success dictate your motivation for the rest of the life. Each and every step is to bring you closer to your ideas and dreams, and when you can clearly notice your upcoming "dream future," you can fully fashion it under your own conditions.

perseverance in the provision of an ultimate crucial goal calls out numerous other virtues in you. You will push yourself to further than what is comfortable to achieve your chosen goal. Furthermore, you should know why you desire your goal in the first place. Plus, your way must be bigger than the difficulties and complications. The bigger the way the better the outcomes, perseverant people have a transparent goal or vision in mind that inspires and induces them. Reaching this ultimate goal becomes the central focal point of their life journey and they devote a larger percentage of their time toward reaching it. If we would like to succeed, we have to pay the price. And the way to success is long with a lot of hurdles and obstacles. No wonder most of the people stop at one point or another after running into the obstacle or barriers. Only the handful of people has this special quality to keep moving forward, and these are some people who succeed.

perseverance is essential. perseverance is probably one of the most worthy and excellent characters a person can possess. It's the ability to be determined to accomplish something regardless of any obstructions and setbacks. Hence, arm yourself with the right state of mind and the right tactics to overcome failure. Perseverance or perseverance is mainly about the basic optimism of knowing your dream is the right thing to chase. In fact, there is no other way to succeed and achieve something huge but by developing perseverance in your life, and here we would also share a few significant ways to develop it.

Do you believe in perseverance?

Aren't you? perseverance is being able to continue a human action until one has succeeded, like winning a race. When you start running, you keep on pushing yourself until you have crossed the finish line. For instance, in special education, having perseverance in teaching a kid until he/she has reached their ultimate goal is like a race. You are perseverant in helping them reach their destination and don't stop until they have reached their objective. People tend to hold on to their beliefs even when it seems that they should not. perseverance is the tendency to cling to one's initial belief even after receiving fresh information that dis-confirms or contradicts or the basis of that belief. Every single person has tried to change somebody's belief, only to have them obdurately remain unchanged. For example, you may have had such debates concerning the abortion, or evolution.

In the plethora of cases, resistance to challenges to belie is defensible and logical. For instance, if you have always done well in racing, getting the third position on some race should not lead you to abandon your belief that you are generally good in the race. However, in the handful of cases, people cling to beliefs that logically should be abandoned, or at least altered. There is overpowering evidence that smoking increases the probability of contracting cancer and that exposure to media violence heightens the likelihood of aggressive behavior. Even, some people strongly deny these scientific facts. People expend considerable mental energy to maintain their opinion when presented with facts that prove them wrong. They will concentrate on experiences that support their point of view merely will ignore any experiences, even their own, that give grounds that they are wrong. They will do the same thing with any other kinds of evidence as well.

Types of Belief of Perseverance

There are three types of belief perseverance exist —1) social impressions 2) self-impressions, and 3) social theories. The first kind of belief consists of beliefs about the self, considering what one believes about his skills and abilities, including body image and social skills. The second type comprises one belief about specific others, for instance, a parent or best friend. The third type comprises mainly what one believes about how the world mainly works, comprising how people act, feel, interact and think. Social theory opinion can be either directly or indirectly learned which means that they can learn through experience as a member or they can be taught. In the first case, children inclined to learn what is expected of them and of others merely by observing and by being a participating member of society. They will learn what it means to be a daughter, a son, a woman, a man, and the behaviors that go with these different roles. In the second case, persons are taught what to believe. They may be taught by their parents or at school, at church.

When it comes to attaining your objectives or creating change in your life if perhaps won't be simple. You may have to struggle. It will likely take a longer time period than you expect. It is almost certain that you will have short-term failures and setbacks along the way. Particularly, when it involves developing new skills, forming a new resolution, creating new habits, or learning new concepts. Now, the good news, struggle, setbacks, battles, and short-term obstacles do not have to drain your motivation. They do not have to make you want to quit before you have put in enough effort and time to accomplish your goal. In fact, psychologists who study motivation and accomplishment say it could be just the opposite; as long as you adopt the right path and the right mindset. According to my raids of research through decades, there are two fundamental belief systems, also called as "mindsets," that evaluate how people respond to setbacks, struggle, obstacles, and failure when pursuing their goals. In one mindset, you are most likely to get discouraged and give up on your ultimate goal. In the other, you tend to embrace the battle and struggle, learn from the hardship or hurdles and keep moving forward to attain your goals– you persevere.

The science of perseverance: Determined Mindset vs Growth Mindset

What do you believe about human calibers, such as intelligence, talent, and creativeness? If you have adopted a "fixed mindset," you view them as traits that you are either born with, or not, and it is not much you can do to alter it. On the flip side, if you have adopted a "growth mindset," you see them as capacities that you can develop through determination, practice, education, and hard work.

How about character traits like grit, willpower, and self-discipline? With a fixed mindset, you believe attributes like these are mostly static and predetermined by your genes and fostering – either you have them or you do not. Through the lens of a growth mindset, you see them as malleable skills that you can prepare, gear up and strengthen over the course of your life (even science also proves this to be true).

In a fixed mindset, people believe their basic attributes, like their intelligence, ability, or talent, are just fixed traits. They spend their time on the piece of writing their intelligence or talent instead of developing them. They also accept the fact that talent alone creates success; without excessive effort. They are actually wrong. On the flip side, in a growth mindset, people believe that their most basic qualities can be developed through dedication, commitment, and hard work. This view creates a love of learning and a resilience that is necessary for great achievement. Virtually all great people have had these calibers. Teaching a growth mindset creates productivity and motivation in the worlds of education, business, and sports. It deepens relationships. When you read Mindset, you will see how.

Fixed Mindset Weakens Your Dedication

Our mind is a meaning-making machine. Whether you are aware of it or not, you are continuously monitoring what is happening around you, understanding what it means and deciding what to do about it. This is apparently the significant procedure for your survival, but it is also the main driver of all your suffering – particularly when it is molded by the fixed mindset. When you struggle hardship or fail to attain your ultimate objectives, you make that mean something about yourself. In the fixed mindset, this mainly means you are simply not good enough, or that you for some reason do not have what it takes. For instance, have you ever thought or said things like: I'm not creative, I don't have any self-discipline, I have no talent, I'm not good with new technology, It's hard for me to lose the extra pound, I'm shy, I am not athletic, etc. It is healthy to acknowledge your limitations and recognize where you can be doing better in your life. But that's not what's happening in the fixed mindset. Remember, the fixed mindset believes that abilities and talent are mainly fixed and preset – either you have it, or don't. If you have, great. If not, why even why bother to try? You might as well give up, and keep move on to something simpler. Perhaps, this is not the kind of thinking that helped the big personalities like J.K. Rowling and Stephen King become bestselling authors. It is not the kind of thinking that creates motivation to persevere when the going gets tough.

Growth Mindset Fortifies Your Motivation

The growth mindset interprets failure and challenging situations much differently than the fixed mindset. Just remember, the core opinion of the growth mindset is that human powers and talents are malleable skills that you can set up and strengthen over the course of your life. The fixed mindset erroneously views your limitations as permanent. On the other hand, the growth mindset understands they are just a starting turning point – guiding stars that tell you where to spend your energy toward professional and personal development. The growth mindset is an antidote to defeatism. It interprets challenge & failure, not as a signal to throw in the towel, however, as a healthy and natural part of human growing and accomplishment.

This might sound like a good old-fashioned or outdated positive thinking, and maybe it is. The difference of opinion is these conclusions are based on 40 years of stringent, scientific research – more than hundreds of studies that all say similar facts. If you want to strengthen your motivation, accomplish your goals and lead a more fulfilling life, you are best served by a growth mindset. You now have a choice with regard to how you interpret struggle, failure, and setbacks. You can interpret it from a fixed mindset as proof that you are somehow not cut out to win. Or you can interpret it from a growth mindset as guidance for where to keep your focus on your efforts toward personal & professional development. Most perseverance research on naive theories has focused on beliefs about people and how they feel, behave, think, and interact and other social theories. Examples include stereotypes about teenagers, Muslims, Asian Americans; beliefs about artists, lawyers, firefighters; even beliefs about the causes of poverty, violence or war.

Early belief perseverance studies tested whether individuals often truly cling to unfounded viewpoints more so than is logically justifiable. However, it is complex and tricky to specify just how much a given belief "should" modify in response to fresh and New Testament. One "C Grade" on a math test should not completely overwhelm other years of "A"s in other math classes, however, how much transform (if any) is warranted? There is one clear and apparent case in which researchers can state how much belief change should happen. That case is when the basis of a precise belief is totally dishonored or discredited. For instance, imagine that John tells Maria that the new team member is not very active. Maria may even meet and interact with the new member for several days before learning that John was actually speaking about a different new joiner. Because Maria knows that his initial belief about new member's intelligence was based on completely irrelevant information, Maria's impression about the new joiner should now be totally uninfluenced by John's initial statement. This, in essence, describes the debriefing paradigm, the primary technique used to study unwarranted belief perseverance. In the first belief perseverance revision using this way, partially half of the research participant members were led to suppose and believe that they had performed fine on a social perceptiveness task; the rest half were led to judge that they had performed badly. Afterward, all were told that their performance had been manipulated by the researcher to see how participant members take action and respond to failure or success. Participants were even shown the paper sheet that listed their name and whether they were thought to be given failure or success feedback. Later, participants had to guess how well they really did and foresee how well they would do in the future on this assigned task or job.

Logically, those in the initial failure and success situations should not differ in their self-beliefs about their future or actual performance on this social perceptiveness job, for the reason that early beliefs based on the fake feedback should revert to their normal level once it was exposed that the feedback was faked. Nevertheless, participants who received fake success feedback constantly believe that they were pretty good at this task, while those who received fake failure comment perseverantly believe that they were pretty bad at it. Other studies of social impressions and self-impressions have found parallel effects concerning distinct beliefs.

The initial study of social theory perseverance used the same debriefing paradigm to find out whether fictitious info about the relation between the personality attribute "riskiness" and firefighter quality could create a persevere social theory. Though, after debriefing about the fictitious nature of the first information, participants at the start led to believe that risky people make finer firefighters and those initially led to believe that high-risk people make poorer firefighters persist in their initial beliefs. At least there are three psychological procedures underlie belief perseverance. One refers to use of the "availability heuristic" for deciding what is most liable to happen. When judging your own power at a specific task, you are likely to try to recollect memory how good you have done on similar tasks in the past, that is, how available (in memory) are past successful versus failures. However, whether you recall more failures or successes critically depends on galore factors, such as how memorable the several occasions were and how often you have actually thought about them, but not inevitably on how often you have failed or succeeded. The second activity concerns "illusory correlation," wherein one sees or remembers more confirmed cases and few dis confirming cases than really subsist. The third procedure concerns "data distortions," wherein dis confirming cases are neglected and confirming cases are inadvertent. For instance, if you are told that a new team member is rude, you are more likely to treat that individual in a way that invites rudeness or discourtesy and to forget instances of politeness. Research also has examined ways to belief perseverance. The most obvious answer, asking people to be unbiased, does not work, nevertheless, various techniques to reduce the problem. The most successful is to get the individual to imagine or explain how the other belief might be true. This DE-biasing technique is referred to as the counter explanation.

Varied Types

There are three extraordinary kinds of belief perseverance, viz.

Social impressions

Self-impressions

Naive theories

Social Impressions

Social Impressions bring up to the beliefs that people have about others. These could be supported on a one-time, previous experience (either positive or negative) that people have about others and shape an opinion, which leads into forming an opinion. These can be formed with just about any individual.

Self-impressions

Self-impressions mention to the beliefs that we harbor about ourselves. These have to do with our belief about our confidence, athletic skills, body image, academic inescapable, musical knowledge, and the like. This belief system considers both negative and positive beliefs. For instance, somebody might be a good public speaker, however, he/ she has a strong belief that he cannot speak in the public place, and it cannot be shaken in spite of people complimenting him. The mistaken belief like this one can have severe consequences and can lead to a skewed perspective of oneself. On the other hand, an exaggerated view of someone can also lead to problems.

Naive Theories

Such impressions are based on someone's belief about how the world works. Naive theories mostly correspond with social theories—the belief about folks, how they behave, think, and interact with others. Naive theories go on to comprise major stereotypes steeped in the society that has to do with the handful of issues about communities, religion, teen, professions, and other beliefs that may even comprise what gives rise to poorness, causes of war, and violence, and the like.

Chapter Two

Keep going until you are successful

Holding on to set beliefs and speculations based on unwarranted data and in the light of conflicting evidence, demonstrates that conviction perseverance exists, as well as that our conviction framework isn't just shaped based on certainties and sensible data, however to an expansive degree on how we feel about ourselves, about others, and about other general theories and hypotheses. Despite the fact that this unwavering belief can help from numerous points of view, most different occasions, it shapes a boundary which keeps us from settling on the correct decisions. Illustration of a similar will be featured in the accompanying area.

Examples

Positive Example-You're a brilliant cook and individuals dependably compliment you on your dishes. Yet, on one specific event, you happen to burn the sandwich you're cooking; this does not imply that you're an awful cook or that you need to scrutinize your conviction about being a decent cook. For this situation, the belief perseverance has enabled you to restore your confidence in your cooking and continue.

Negative Examples-However, there are occasions when belief perseverance goes about as a hurdle. For instance, a man has met with 4 accidents during a span of a month, but, he keeps on trusting that he is a superb driver. Or then again suppose that your companion has been dating a person who treats her badly, and whilst everybody around her can see this and have been revealing to her the same, she basically declines to say a final breakup to him since she trusts he loves her as too, and he will change.

In the two instances, the individual does not take cognizance of anything that repudiates his/her belief system, which at that point negatively affects his life, since he can't take logical conclusion or judgment.

Why perseverance significant in our Life?

perseverance is the essences of accelerating your prospects of being successful in a specific thing or accomplishing a specific objective, and it likewise can assist you with staying motivated and continue striving towards the one long haul objective you want to achieve. For instance, when you first started your company, you most likely had dreams of success and recognition. You were positive that sales were reaching to pour in, and you'd be busy creating a great deal of cash. When you truly operated your company, it most likely dawned upon you rather quickly that hopes, visions, and dreams alone weren't sufficient. Starting a business taught you that being a business owner isn't as simple as you once thought it might be. In fact, it's a great deal of labor with little reward gained at the outset. This is the reason why business failure rates are thus high. Folks merely cannot overcome the roadblocks and demands that accompany entrepreneurship.

The one word that may be used to describe businessperson who succeeds at business ownership is 'perseverant'. You need to be perseverant if you would like to be ready to sustain your business through the challenges and hurdles of entrepreneurship and sooner or later reap the rewards of a successful business. The truth is that Entrepreneurship comes with loads of ups and downs. Typically it feels as if you expertise a lot of downs than ups as you're within the early stages of business development. This is often once your mental attitude needs to stay optimistic and tough if you're getting to go through the hardships of constructing your business. If you're presently having a tough time in your business, you'd get advantage from reading some quotes regarding perseverance. These quotes can assist you to understand that you simply aren't the sole one who has undergone troubles as a business owner. Others are through what you're presently going through and possibly abundantly worse. But, they still built successful businesses despite their hurdles as a result of they remained to persevere.

 The definition of perseverance is once you are desperate to do one thing considerably and not permitting anyone or any troubles stop you for doing it. This definition couldn't be any length suitable which is what the beauty of determination is and why it's therefore vital for anyone to have. With zero determination, it can lead you to give up on the single thing that you just needed to try to due to the issue that you just faced with or what somebody else has same. Nobody ought to ever surrender on one thing that they really need to try to as a result of everybody can achieve something if they are willing to place in the work a strong mindset towards overcoming the particular challenge and overcoming people that disagree and create trouble and don't have your best interest to your life.

Why perseverance is significant than planning?

We are mysterious creatures. Anguish and hope can coexist and still create something astonishing. Perseverance is the ability to maintain action despite your feelings. It has a lot to do with your life's success and business success. It is considered as an omnipotent. An American politician Calvin Coolidge once stated "The slogan "press on" has solved and always will solve the troubles of the human race". Intelligence and ability cannot take the place of perseverance. The worth of perseverance comes from a visualization of the future that is so compelling you would give approx anything to make it factual or real. perseverance of action draws closer from the perseverance of vision. When you are specifically clear about what you want in such a way that your vision does not change much, you will be more unfailing and perseverant in your dealings. Hence, that consistency of action will produce consistency of outcomes. One favorite quote state that "no plan survives first contact with the enemy." We have learned this reality time and time again. Mike Tyson put it well when he stated, "Everybody has an arrangement until the point when they get punched in the face." Regular arranging is basic to maintain a business yet we find that readiness and steadiness are significantly more imperative that the most ideal marketable strategy. Clear emergency courses of action were basic for mission achievement.

 Here are reasons that being well-prepared and perseverant to tackle life's obstruction is significant than trying to manage things out of your control.

Things do not generally go as planned, thus be ready when the inevitable obstruction or hurdles stand in your way. Whether you are the team member of the big-giant corporation or an entrepreneur growing a start-up, you have probably noticed that plans can change, and change often. But the enterprise has to be well-structured to remain dynamic, robust and strong. Good leaders must continue focused on what lays ahead for foreseeing potential blockage and adjust accordingly. Experiencing letdown along your path to accomplishment does not mean you failed. Failure generally occurs when you allow those experiences cause you to give up. Planning does not ensure adaptability In the Teams, while doing fight dive training we had a saying, "Plan your dive, & dive your plan." Things can get confusing underwater in pitch blackness, however, when you start second guess yourself, it can snowball uncontrollable. That's why it is said, good old fashion common sense is also a great reserve and stand-in when your plan starts falling apart.

For companies, they must have robust financials, nimble leadership, and a team with a shared sense of purpose. Planning does not identify unknowns. perseverance and obstinacy are what makes companies successful. The character is built during the third and fourth shots at attaining the goal. Not the first try. In trade, there are always myriads of things out of your control like the economy or your client's financial situations. But that's senseless reason to irritate and make knee jerk decisions. You just have to stay calm, cool and positive and try to keep moving. A great quote about perseverance from Martin Luther King Jr. states that "If you can't fly you run if you can't run you walk if you can't walk your crawls. But no matter what, you keep moving forward."

Good plans are valueless without proper implementation. Plus flawless execution takes some practice. You can use up all the time in the world developing big plans for your business but if you do not brag the ability to perform on those plans you will surely fail. There also has to be buy-in across the board for organizations to be effectual at hitting their goals. Never discount the significance of having a proper plan and even better contingency strategies. But you need to keep in mind that if you spend proper time to make sure you have the capability to adapt as required, it won't feel like you are trying to steer a cruise ship when an iceberg placed in your pathway. It is perseverance that keeps you moving forward, having important goals are not achieved overnight, they necessitate, and no they demand patience, perseverance, and perseverance. If you perseverance take action, you will build momentum. "If Columbus had ever thought to turn back, no one would have blamed him. No one would have memorized him either."

 In the face of challenge, perseverance ensures that we continue to take action towards the accomplishment of our objective. As World's famous educationalist points out, this may require us to frequent adjustments to our tactics, until we achieve the objective.

"If you have an important point to make, don't try to be subtle or clever. Use a pile driver. Hit the point once. Then come back and hit it again. Then hit it a third time - a tremendous whack."— Winston S. Churchill

Reflecting on your objectives...

• Do you require amending the strategies you are using to archive your goal?

• Have you persevered toward your objective? Or have you perhaps given up too soon?

There are two mentalities: buckle down and

achieve your objectives, or not bother since you likely won't succeed in any case. In spite of the fact that this may appear to be an oversimplification, we think this oblivious choice has an aggravating impact all through your life. In the event that you are in the camp of "making a decent attempt leads to achievement", you invest more energy, you take rejection in your stride (despite the fact that regardless it harms), you get up every single time you fall, and you feel motivated to attempt and attempt and try again until you succeed. Whether it's a spelling bee or beginning your own organization: trusting you can accomplish something through diligent work is a critical element for success. Be in the other camp of "you won't succeed" paying little heed to what you do, there is an unequivocally negative example. You feel that whatever you do throughout everyday life, you presumably won't succeed in any case, so you don't feel inspired to attempt in any case. When you confront difficulties and hurdles, you see that as a sign that you will fail. When you are rejected, again you feel weak, powerless and unfortunate.

In psychology, there's an idea called "locus of control": an individual's conviction about how long they can control the events around them: do you take control of the things you can control, or do you blame external components for your prosperity or disappointment. Sooner or later the vast majority have most likely identified with both camps. However, we imagine that over the time goes there is a huge exacerbating impact, encountering little hurdles and difficulties and after that success, which inspires you to handle bigger challenges and to feel well prepared for greater misfortunes.

Set your psyche to an objective, something that you believe is bizarre and afterward buckles down to accomplish it. Depending upon the "challenge" you pick – it might take the number of hours or only a week. Learn a language, run more distant than you might suspect you could, and figure out how to cook another dish, get the courage to complete an open talking in Public, climb a mountain, build something, influence something, and create something. Set an objective that scares you a little and drives you out of your comfort zone. The truth is that you have accomplished something that you thought was unimaginable and not possible, you will be raring to go for your next toughest challenge and more resilient to the hindrances that you will unavoidably face out and along the way.

Here are 4 reasons Perseverance is vital to your prosperity and success:

1. PERSEVERANCE HELPS YOU CONQUER THE UNEXPECTED

At the point when things don't work out as expected, it's tempting to surrender. We lose our confidence and consider moving onward to something that is less demanding. This is actually what the vast majorities of people do on the grounds that we're anxious about disappointment or failure and evade far from things that are hard and necessary. Plans make us feel safe, yet be prepared when things turn out of your control so you can land on your feet. You may need to change course and adjust somehow. Your objective continues to be the same as before, however, your road map may need to be changed. Try to develop a nimble mentality by attempting to anticipate potential misfortunes and have an alternate course of action for them.

2. PERSEVERANCE ENABLES YOU TO KEEP FOCUSED

At the point when things turn out badly, it is difficult to keep up motivation and core interest. Perseverance enables you to stay concentrated on long haul objectives so you can change your behavior accordingly. Regularly, this expects you to hold feelings in line to keep emotions in check from sabotaging your endeavors and efforts to continue advancing and moving forward. Visualize yourself achieving your objective regardless of what it takes. Watch out for the objective and see yourself reaching the end.

3. PERSEVERANCE IS FED BY ENCOURAGEMENT AND SUPPORT

At the point when things turn out of your control, discover support and encouragement from people around you whom you trust and respect. In view of their experience and ability, search out their recommendation, suggestions, and proposals on the how to proficiently continue moving ahead. Successful individuals with perseverance comprehend that still need to do the tough work, yet it is extremely encouraging when you are surrounded with positive back up. We in our own island as a whole need other individuals' assistance and support. It may be a short talk or a couple of words of assistance. Be the individual who connects when you require assistance rather than to surrender. Do not be afraid to share your situations with other people, however, be particular about it. Ensure they are individuals who really need what is best for you and will give you both valuable and positive feedback. Seek for "mirror" companions or friends who will be fair, cherishing, honest, and objective.

4. PERSEVERANCE MAKES YOU DIG DEEP DOWN

If you are on a path that has meaning, value, and significance for you, you are unquestionably on the right path, so keep going. If you are not, then a delay or failure will be enough to make you surrender and try something else. Success can be exceptionally misleading on the grounds that frequently it is the place we remain, regardless of whether it's what truly fills us or not. It is a success that is based in complacency because we are too scared of failure to pursue the type of work that would offer worth and meaning. Don't take the easiest path, dig deep down where it counts and discovers the things that you can't leave. When you are pursuing that sort of objective, it won't make any difference what other individuals say on the grounds that your inner vision is far stronger than any external hindrance you will come up against.

Taking everything into account, in short, perseverance is an essential piece of life. Its isolates the complete from the incomplete and just to recap, here are the 5 key reasons why having perseverance satisfies:

• Most successful persons have failed in any event once

• People jump at the chance to test you on the determination

• What comes effectively typically isn't justified, despite any potential benefits

• Knowledge isn't picked up without ingenuity and perseverance

• The more you accomplish something, the better you get at it

Permanence, perseverance, and perseverance in spite of all obstacles, discouragements, and impossibilities: It is this that in all things distinguishes the strong soul from the weak.

Our mind is incredibly powerful (lot more than you imagine) and with a bit of guidance and mind training, you can completely change your frame of mind. What this actually states is that you can pin down all those magical moments that you have stopped noticing while you hunt after the clock, which, unlike you, by no means has to make any stops. Just try to believe in yourself. You cannot uncover beauty outside if you cannot see it inside yourself. If you are always seeking outward approval you are seriously going to lose precious time. And that is the time you could have spent dreaming about your upcoming big projector or developing any new skill you want to be trained. When you start believing in your abilities and yourself, the possibilities become never-ending. You turn into an imaginative and inspired human being, you dare to grow, you dare to dream, you dare to share your dreams with other people, and you lose your terror of being ridiculed for it. Planning. Education. Desire. All these start contributing to your success part but none of them are sufficient without perseverance. – Michael Josephson. Everything starts with a vision, an idea, or yes a dream. The dissimilarity between people who believe in themselves & people who do not is that the people who do believe they will be able to take one step ahead than their strength permits them. And that's when the miracles come into view and they end up triumph no one thought they ever could. "Magic believes in yourself, if you can do that, you can make anything happen." -Johann Wolfgang con Goethe- So, try to get yourself moving. We're all the makers of our own lives. We can act in a lot of dissimilar ways and influence the situations we find ourselves in, and how we take action in all these times will lead to a convincing result.

So it's significant to know what mental state you are in when you are about to take steps. If you are acting from a place of love, understanding, care and, compassion, your actions will surely be graceful, magical, and influential and they will also be part of a better life. When you act out of love you won't very soon feel better, however, you will also inspire other people to do it too. Love always attracts extra love, and that goes way beyond the real results of any action on its own. But if your trials of actions come from your ego, if they have a basis in mistrust, criticism, terror, or suspicion, you'll just attract those similar things. You'll attract a similar type of situations and people over & over again. Now it is the time to change that. Don't be frightened. There is magic waiting for you around the corner, and the finest part is that you can create it. Actually, we have already gone into so many ingredients to create magic, now it's in our hands to magnetize it.

Here are some of the significant things that helped you keep going that day and bring the magic of perseverance in your life when everything in you wanted to quit. If you find yourself in circumstances where you want to stop or give up, these lessons can help you, too.

1. Ignore others- At the beginning of the mountaineering, you can only see the people passing in front of you. Every time you see someone hiking without extra effort, you might feel bad about yourself. But when you stopped comparing and stopped worrying everyone ease's journey to your own, you seriously began to concentrate on your own mission and how you are going to attain it. As you work toward your vision, it can be simple to get distracted when you see others attaining their objectives faster, easier, far better than you. It can make you feel unsatisfied and disappointed with your own progress. But when it comes to vectoring a goal, what's happening with others is extraneous when it detracts from your capability to move forward. When tackling a

hard task, you need each ounce of energy you can muster. Just ensure to channel it to the right place that will propel you forward.

2. Become your own biggest follower- When you start climbing, you weren't alone. But within 10 minutes, you could be behind and alone. At first, you might be frustrated your companions abandoned you in your time of need. But then you could realize your burden was not theirs to bear. Even though it can be energizing to have others around to encourage and assist you, having them there is a luxury, not a necessity. That lesson allowed you to turn inward and find in yourself the strength, perseverance, and willpower to keep going. You began to encourage and high-five yourself with every single step. Sometimes on the path to victory, you have to walk alone. If you find yourself in that similar position, just find a way to give yourself what you need to carry on.

3. Try to appreciate the small things- You began the trek before the sun was up. As you continued to mount, it started to peek around the mountain, giving glimpses of the sparkling

beauty all around you. It could be miraculous. During the catch-your-breath breaks, you marveled at the privilege of seeing the natural world in all her beauty. In those moments, you gave no thought to your struggle. You could be too busy being gratifying for being right there. It can be simple to focus all your energy on reaching your ultimate objective. But if the only thing you can see is your end purpose, you will miss the beauty of the trip along the way. The new experiences and welcome surprises give you much-required fuel to keep going.

4. Focus on the next step- It can discourage you to think how far away you are from the top. So you might re frame your vision into mini-milestones that made the next steps more manageable. Simply take one more step, you thought. OK, now simply get over to those tough stones. And yes once you get to that the track you can stop and rest for a few minutes. When your objectives seem too big, it can feel impossible, which opens the path for resistance to creep in. By breaking your goal into bite-sized pieces, you can keep yourself in motion, perseverance and build momentum.

5. Lastly, you can try avoiding your watch- Before the trek; you read that there are so many people make it to the top of the mountain in about 45-60 minutes. But it took you so long. When you focused on the time it was supposed to take, you might get frustrated at yourself for not being fast or good enough. But no one cared how long it took me to hike and get to the top and you should not have, either. All that mattered was finishing your journey. As you work on accomplishing your goals, stop looking at the clock. Stop calculating yourself against something or somebody else. It will only serve to distract you from concentrating on what you require to do right now to advance.

6. Stop looking for a way out- Not everybody who goes to mountaineering or hikes. You can easily take a bus straight to the top & save yourself the physical and emotional tension. Early on in your climb, you might think about retreating or waving down the bus on their way up. When your pain is at the forefront, it is normal to want to make it go away. However, when you spend time seeking a way to abort

your journey, you waste valuable energy that could be used to help you conquer momentary pain and distress for long-term growth.

7. Acknowledge your limitations- You had to be honest with yourself. You were having difficulty getting air and you could not keep the pace of the group. Simply, pushing your body to the limit by trying to keep a speedy pace was not going to work for you. Your path needed to be diverse, and that's OK. After implementing your new tactic, the journey was less exhausting. Your path to success might not look like everybody ease's. That's OK. Everybody's situation is poles apart. Instead, acknowledge where you are, so you can offer yourself what you require to be thriving. As you work to attain your objectives, there will be obstructions, bumps, blockages, and bruises along the way. When the journey becomes more painful than what you are used to, it can be simple to throw in the towel & retreat. However, if you follow these lessons, you can find the power to keep going in the midst of complexity. And when you persevere, you will discover the reward was worth the effort. Just so not give up.

As you grow old, you realize that there are real-life strengths that push you to be successful in life and your preferred career and profession.

Our mindset is incredibly influential (lot more than you imagine) and with a bit of guidance and mind training, you can completely change your frame of mind. What this actually states is that you can pin down all those magical moments that you have stopped noticing while you hunt after the clock, which, unlike you, by no means has to make any stops. Just try to believe in yourself. You cannot uncover beauty outside if you cannot see it inside yourself. If you are always seeking outward approval you are seriously going to lose precious time. And that is the time you could have spent dreaming about your upcoming big projector or developing any new skill you want to be trained. When you start believing in your abilities and yourself, the possibilities become never-ending. You turn into an imaginative and inspired human being, you dare to grow, you dare to dream, you dare to share your dreams with other people, and you lose your terror of being ridiculed for it. Plan and desire start contributing to your success part but none of them are sufficient without perseverance. – Michael Josephson. Everything starts with a vision, an idea, or yes a dream. The dissimilarity between people who believe in themselves & people who do not is that the people who do believe they will be able to take one step ahead than their strength permits them. And that's when the miracles come into view and they end up triumph no one thought they ever could. "Magic believes in yourself, if you can do that, you can make anything happen." -Johann Wolfgang von Goethe- So, try to get yourself moving. We're all the makers of our own lives. We can act in a lot of dissimilar ways and influence the situations we find ourselves in, and how we take action in all these times will lead to a convincing result.

So it's significant to know what mental state you are in when you are about to take steps. If you are acting from a place of love, understanding, care and, compassion, your actions will surely be graceful, magical, and influential and they will also be part of a better life. When you act out of love you won't very soon feel better, however, you will also inspire other people to do it too. Love and affection always draw towards extra affection, and that goes way beyond the real results of any act on its own. But if your trials of actions come from your ego, if they have a basis in mistrust, criticism, terror, or suspicion, you'll just attract those similar things. You'll attract a similar type of situations and people over & over again. Now it is the time to change that. Don't be frightened. There is magic waiting for you around the corner, and the finest part is that you can create it. Actually, we have already gone into so many ingredients to create magic, now it's in our hands to magnetize it.

Here are some of the significant things that helped you keep going that day and bring the magic of perseverance in your life when everything in you wanted to quit. If you find yourself in circumstances where you want to stop or give up, these lessons can help you, too.

1. Ignore others- At the beginning of the mountaineering, you can only see the people passing in front of you. Every time you see

someone hiking without extra effort, you might feel bad about yourself. But when you stopped comparing and stopped worrying everyone else's journey to your own, you seriously began to concentrate on your own mission and how you are going to attain it. As you work toward your vision, it can be simple to get distracted when you see others attaining their objectives faster, easier, far better than you. It can make you feel unsatisfied and disappointed with your own progress. But when it comes to vectoring a goal, what's happening with others is extraneous when it detracts from your capability to move forward. When tackling a hard task, you need each ounce of energy you can muster. Just ensure to channel it to the right place that will propel you forward.

2. Become your own biggest follower- When you start climbing, you weren't alone. But within 10 minutes, you could be behind and alone. At first, you might be frustrated your companions abandoned you in your time of need. But then you could realize your burden was not theirs to bear. Even though it can be energizing to have others around to encourage

and assist you, having them there is a luxury, not a necessity. That lesson allowed you to turn inward and find in yourself the strength, perseverance, and willpower to keep going. You began to encourage and high-five yourself with every single step. Sometimes on the path to victory, you have to walk alone. If you find yourself in that similar position, just find a way to give yourself what you need to carry on.

3. Try to appreciate the small things- You began the trek before the sun was up. As you continued to mount, it started to peek around the mountain, giving glimpses of the sparkling beauty all around you. It could be miraculous. During the catch-your-breath breaks, you marveled at the privilege of seeing the natural world in all her beauty. In those moments, you gave no thought to your struggle. You could be too busy being gratifying for being right there. It can be simple to focus all your energy on reaching your ultimate objective. But if the only thing you can see is your end purpose, you will miss the beauty of the trip along the way. The new experiences and welcome surprises give you much-required fuel to keep going.

4. Focus on the next step- It can discourage you to think how far away you are from the top. So you might reframe your vision into mini-milestones that made the next steps more manageable. Simply take one more step, you thought. OK, now simply get over to those tough stones. And yes once you get to that the track you can stop and rest for a few minutes. When your objectives seem too big, it can feel impossible, which opens the path for resistance to creep in. By breaking your goal into bite-sized pieces, you can keep yourself in motion, perseverance and build momentum.

5. Lastly, you can try avoiding your watch- Before the trek; you read that there are so many people make it to the top of the mountain in about 45-60 minutes. But it took you so long. When you focused on the time it was supposed to take, you might get frustrated at yourself for not being fast or good enough. But no one cared how long it took me to hike and get to the top and you should not have, either. All that mattered was finishing your journey. As you work on accomplishing your goals, stop looking at the clock. Stop

calculating yourself against something or somebody else. It will only serve to distract you from concentrating on what you require to do right now to advance.

6. Stop looking for a way out- Not everybody who goes to mountaineering or hikes. You can easily take a bus straight to the top & save yourself the physical and emotional tension. Early on in your climb, you might think about retreating or waving down the bus on their way up. When your pain is at the forefront, it is normal to want to make it go away. However, when you spend time seeking a way to abort your journey, you waste valuable energy that could be used to help you conquer momentary pain and distress for long-term growth.

7. Acknowledge your limitations- You had to be honest with yourself. You were having difficulty getting air and you could not keep the pace of the group. Simply, pushing your body to the limit by trying to keep a speedy pace was not going to work for you. Your path needed to be diverse, and that's OK. After implementing your new tactic, the journey was less exhausting.

Your path to success might not look like everybody else's. That's OK. Everybody's situation is poles apart. Instead, acknowledge where you are, so you can offer yourself what you require to be thriving. As you work to attain your objectives, there will be obstructions, bumps, blockages, and bruises along the way. When the journey becomes more painful than what you are used to, it can be simple to throw in the towel & retreat. However, if you follow these lessons, you can find the power to keep going in the midst of complexity. And when you persevere, you will discover the reward was worth the effort. Just so not give up.

As you grow old, you realize that there are real-life strengths that push you to be successful in life and your preferred career and profession.

- Creativity
- Charisma
- Physical abilities
- Cognitive control
- Artistic talent
- And even charisma

So, the harsh truth that most of us countenance at some point in our lives is that we are not the strongest, prettiest, smartest, fastest, or most talented person in the room. Does that mean you are doomed and will never outrageously succeed in your career? No, not at all. It does mean that you need the perfect plan and strategy that doesn't depend on innate talent to carry the day.

There is hope- Some of you know that you are remarkably talented, gorgeous, superstars, super genius. If so, you do not need any advice and you do not need anybody's help. You are already ruling the earth. Go in peace, follow the magic of perseverance my friends. Now, for those who are still in search and want to know the secret, rest assured: there is hope for the rest of your life. Perhaps there are few among us who will admit that they are in this group of hope conception. You may not always be the most talented, smartest, and most imaginative person in the room. However, you can tap into these three superpowers and still attain great success in your life, love, and career.

You simply need to be:

- Consistent
- Resistant
- perseverant

You just do not mean to have perseverant, resistant, and consistent traits. You also need to exhibit heroic levels of each. But, the great news is that anybody can do this if they are truly ambitious, dedicated, willing, and as stubborn as famous personalities like Steve Jobs.

- **Consistent**

You create new habits easily and you are consistent with those habits. James Clear has an excellent story on this. Process beats goal sets. Systems will hit vision. Try to concentrate more on what you will consistently do each day and you will achieve more than dreaming about what you want. As people fall in love with planning and goals, and then they get discouraged when things went wrong (as they always do in the end). Or, they want the outcomes, but they really do not want to constantly put in the hard work required. Fall in love with the everyday procedure and enjoy the journey. The outcomes are a side effect. They are nice, of course. It is fun to celebrate the victories along the way. The truth is when you truly start loving the process you will tolerate the hard times and setbacks. The failure here or there does not destroy you. You become overcharged and perseverance work as bulletproof. Keep on, move on and you cannot help but see great results. "We are what we repeatedly do. Excellence, then, is not an act, but a habit." —Aristotle

- **Resistant**

Resistance is the right word for "extremely stubborn." If somebody tells you that you cannot do anything, you should prove them wrong by doing it. Maybe you will even do it twice (like mundane events). If somebody tells you that you must do something, it fuels your willpower and drives to never do that thing. But, more often than not, it may push you or enable you to accomplish things that shouldn't have been possible for someone like you. Or, at least that is what you were told. I was told that I was too poor to go to college.

How many times has someone told you that you weren't good enough to do something? It wasn't because they are willing to spend their lives that way. Just follow the magic of perseverance and resist anyone who tells you what you can and can't do with your life. They do not have an idea or know the drive or fire that you have inside. They do not completely understand what you are capable of doing if you persevere. They don't have to live your life. Only you have to. So, "Don't let others define you. You define yourself."—Ginni Rometty

- **perseverant**

"We don't get a chance to do that many things, and everyone should be really excellent. Because this is our life"—*Steve Jobs.*

When you are trying to solve a problem or learn something new, you should refuse to give up. You get tunnel vision and you can persist until you get it done, one way or the different ways. Daniel Goleman would call this "Grit" and he considered that it is the biggest predictors of your success. It does not for all time mean that the solution needs to come from me. Sometimes it means that you hire or take assistance from someone who can provide you the solution. But, you should persist until it is done. Just be stubborn, try the magical perseverance and refuse to give up or be stopped. This is a magical superpower that only a few have. But now you can easily try and can do this! Anybody can be perseverant, set their sights on something, and keep grinding to make it happen. You do not fully agree with every aspect of but, you can believe in the philosophy of perseverance.

"Nothing in this world can take the place of perseverance. Talent will not: nothing is more common than unsuccessful men with talent. Genius will not; unrewarded genius is almost a proverb. Education will not: the world is full of educated derelicts. perseverance and determination alone are omnipotent."— Calvin Coolidge

You might have a boatload of knowledge, talent, skills, and experience. Everybody does, in their own approach. But, don't worry if you are not the absolute best at everything. Be consistent, perseverant, and resistant. Those superpowers are accessible to all of us. Inherent talent can only take you so far. However, the big three will take you the rest of the way. *Permanence, perseverance, and perseverance in spite of all obstacles, discouragements and impossibilities: It is this that in all things distinguishes the strong soul from the weak.-Thomas Carlyle*

perseverance is where you get mental strength. Perseverance and determination will carve you as a leader in your industry. It makes you extraordinary and separates you from normal people. You must learn to cultivate a habit of perseverance since everything is possible if you persevere. The perseverant man or woman does not accept defeat, he just keeps climbing on it. It has incredible magic and power. To reach the zenith tower, if we took one step at a time and continue to take slow and steady steps and not stop. People of greatness have finished the race for success while encountering all the hurdles that are hurled their way, which generally deters common people. Perseverance is a crucial step on your path, to reach your dream. People, in order to live to his fullest potential, must have a vision. To reach that goal you must build your own route. The first step is willpower and the second is dedication, the third is the positive attitude and the fourth is discipline, and the final step is the most imperative being perseverant. "Some people have greatness thrust upon them. Very few have excellence thrust upon them." –John W. Gardner

The individual with determination and perseverance will succeed over the person with extra talent, more money or higher education. Nothing can replace perseverance not talent nor education, neither genius. Lack of perseverance is a weak spot which filters all the way through a majority of the races. perseverance can turn hardship into greatness. Read Autobiographies and Biographies of famous personalities. Follow some of the principles they had engaged to succeed. You can make the right choice today. Focus on the kind of result you want to produce. Set the target for this year. Set tools to work with, to attain this target. Fall in love with your dream and discipline your life. Remember all great people started as average human beings but had a passion, dream, persisted, endured, strong-minded, disciplined, devoted and with a positive mental attitude attained their goals. If they can persist, so you can, so embark on to persist.

Winston Saga is one of the world's leading

sales legends. He is also the CEO of Sales and Motivation International. Winston has been acknowledged as a unique and distinctive authority in the field of sales and personal development. Last year International Biography Centre selected him "International Man of the Year" for his outstanding contribution to sales and Service. He has written 100's of articles to magazine, journals and websites. If you're going through hell, keep going. — Winston Churchill

If you are seriously going to attain excellence in big things, you develop the habit in little matters. Brilliance is not an exception; it is a prevailing approach and attitude.

Chapter 5

The Power of perseverance

Just believe in yourself even others do not. If you are not at the level you need to be, discover a means to make yourself better. "I've failed over and over and over again in my life. And that is why I succeed." – Michael Jordan. Ever one craves success. But simply waiting for it, however, would not guarantee success and achievement. That is the key reasons why there are so many people fail to attain their goal: They encounter adversity, suffering, and give up. So let's discuss one characteristic required to achieve what you set out to do: perseverance is the blend of powerful desire and determination. Once upon a time, a person named Paul encountered tremendous obstacles like physical punishment, shipwreck, constant danger, etc., but he chooses never to quit. What motivated Paul to persist amidst struggles? He had a clear goal and trusted that his strong willpower would enable him to achieve it. Paul had his eyes fixed on his ultimate purpose, which he so valued that no situation could deter him. At the end of the day, he achieved what had ordained. Just like the Father have great goals for his kids. Striving for anything less will neither accomplish his nor achieve what he has intended in his life. Once your direction is obvious and clear, you should passionately pursue those goals with the strength and proper guidance—especially when hardship and obstacles arise.

Do not give up! It's how you rise from a collapse that truly defines you as a strong person. For instance the Basketball legend Michael Jordan knows a lot about perseverance and determination. Discussing his stellar career he once illustrated that he had lost almost 300 games and had even missed more than 9 thousand shots. On 26 occasions when he had been hand over with the game-winning shot he had flunked, stated Michael Jordan, "I've failed over and over and over again in my life and that's why I succeed." Eventually, the fact is he succeeded because he persevered. He persisted. He wasn't ready to be a quitter. So, no matter how many times he was fouled (and he was considered one of the most fouled players in the sport's history) he got up and kept going. We can all learn from him and his never quitting perception. perseverance truly pays and makes a way out. One historical classic example you have almost certainly heard and encounter before is that of famous personality-Thomas Edison who said that when developing the electric light bulb he hadn't quit and failed—he had just found 10,000 ways that did not work. Thomas Edison was a veritable and most admired quote machine on the subject of perseverance. He also said, "Many of life's failures are people who did not realize how close they were to success when they gave up." And, "Genius is one percent inspiration, 99% perspiration." perseverance. Perspiration. Dogged determination. These are important traits that go a long way in the business world. The majority of the entrepreneurs in their journey to ultimate success occasionally stumbles and now and then takes serious falls. But, like Edison and Jordan, they keep on going for the reason that they know that they have to endure rejection and failure if they want to become the finest in their respective fields of endeavor. If they want to come out on zenith level.

Since the earliest days of his career when he

started his passion for the game, he might have encountered obstacles large and small. He overcame them all and continues to do so because of the power of perseverance in him, which gave him more confidence, personality, passion, and conviction so that he never give up. Often the only obvious difference between losers and winners is perseverance. Losers fold their cards when hardship enters their lives. However, winners never ever give up. Believe in yourself and be prepared to get your skates on. According to research around 75-80 % of all sales, for instance, take place between the fifth and twelfth probability of contact. Just think about that. Just think, how many people are willing to ask for the sale fifth, six, seven, eight times or else more? Majority of them give up by that stage. You have to bear in your mind—whether you are trying to make a sale, plan a trip, prepare for the competitive exams, or achieve anything else in life's great journey—that every time someone says "no" it is just one step closer to somebody saying "yes."

Can anyone develop the power of perseverance? Of course, they can. It's one of those great abilities that lie inside all of us. You have a mindset and brain to use. You just have to be confident and to take a leap of faith. You simply have to put them into action. It doesn't matter how capable you are, it is not going to get you anywhere in life without perseverance and willpower. Being determined also means being able to develop a thick skin and handle things when it doesn't go your way. Being able to "stick with it" and keep on moving in your journey with the confidence that when one dream ends a shining new dream is just beginning. It is the magic of the cosmos. Being perseverant critically means to overcome any fears that might be holding you back. Fear of making blunders, fear of failure, fear of breakdown, and as well as fear of rejection. Make the bold and strong decision to doggedly pursue your goals. It is the only means you will reach your final destination. Being perseverant and determined logically means being willing to do extra and do it more often than the average person would. You go to one more meeting. You can make extra efforts. You make that one last business deals or sales call just before finishing for the day. Conduct more research than your colleagues. Take a course that will advance your career. Push yourself to learn something new. Successful people persist in going the extra mile. They never stop dreaming about the next attempt that will take them to the stars. So, being perseverant means being relentless. Never give up. Never surrender. The power of perseverance will get you the ultimate prize while others fall by the wayside. As a wise person once said, "You may be dissatisfied if you fail, but you are more destined if you never try at all."

Being perseverant and determined is the one thing which isolates the champs from the failures. At the point when an individual makes up his or her mind to achieve a specific accomplishment and set their focus toward that path, declining to be stopped, he or she normally gets what they followed. The intensity of perseverance, even notwithstanding difficulty, is the true traits of champions. For sure, the individuals who accomplish incredible things are the individuals who don't realize when to stop. From others, they hear insulting comments and critics continually remind them, over again and again, that what they are endeavoring to do, won't work. However, they continue to persevere.

Advice from good-natured companions and alliances to take their misfortunes like a man or lady does not dissuade the true winner in life. Stopping isn't in the vocabulary of success and powerful individuals. Finding another approach to achieve objectives is fine. Searching for alternate paths to a similar destiny is okay. In any case, to the challenge and courage of heart, there is no such reality as stopping. Being relentless is the one thing which isolates the victors from the losers. At the point when an individual makes up his or her mind to achieve a specific feat and set their concentration toward that path, declining to be deterred, he or she typically gets what they followed.

The principle is simple but significant. It has made winners out of many and keeps on doing as such. Apply this principle and you will taste the sweetness of triumph. Live by this principle and you will experience accomplishment again and again. Instruct this experience with other people and you will experience success over and over again. Being in presence works in this principle to perfection. This principle is in pretty much every achievement book ever written. A portion of those who lived by this principle saw its astonishing outcomes, determined to share what they learned, through their compositions. Unfortunately, numerous individuals don't invest in their books to take in a win rule or success principle that is old, but then new, for each time an individual activates the principle, the outcome in that individual's life is new, sweet, and ground-breaking. The principle is simple: know what you need, you will have what you need, and seek after it perseverantly, until the point when you get it.

Would it be able to be that simple, some may inquire? Is that really the way to progress? The response is a resounding YES. We challenge you to read after those who have accomplished an extraordinary proportion of achievement and check whether they didn't apply this principle. It will be proven genuine that if you are perseverant in a good thing, and you decline to stop, sooner or later, what you seek after will find you. "Nothing on the planet can replace perseverance. Talent won't, Capability won't, and nothing is more common than failed men with talent and capability. Education won't; the world is laden with educated derelicts. Genius won't; unrewarded Genius is like a proverb. Constancy and perseverance alone are omnipotent. The motto 'Go ahead' has solved and will take care of the issues of the human race." The conventional definition of perseverance is: "Declining to surrender or given up; persevering resolutely; firm or constant perseverance in a course of action despite struggle." Is any person wonder then, that perseverance is the fundamental principal and distinction between successful results and unsuccessful results? In that case, it behooves us to build up the essential traits of determination and perseverance.

If you're going through hell, keep going. – Winston Churchill. What about Colonel Sanders, the founder of Kentucky Fried Chicken? He was a military retiree and had nothing to his name, aside from his mom's chicken recipe formula. So what did he do? He took his old sports wagon out and started driving to many restaurants after restaurant after restaurant. His purpose was to offer the Chicken recipe formula, yet he was turned down consistently, multiple times 1,007 times before he received his first yes. That one yes is the thing that made Kentucky Fried Chicken possible. We keep going with story after story of those who had to be adaptable, imaginative, flexible, and above all perseverant regardless of failing hundreds, sometimes a large number of times. You can also learn from Steve Jobs. He's had had movies made about his story, so you are likely more comfortable with the difficulties and challenges he faced in becoming one of the success and wealthiest corporations on the planet. Members of his own board of directors betrayed him out of his own business. He could have enabled this to stop him; but instead, he chooses to come back to Apple and voted back in as the Apple's Chairman. He created the iPhone, the iPod, and the fresh line of Mac Laptops. Businesses today are incomprehensible without your iPhone.

The three great essentials to achieve anything worthwhile are, first, hard work; second, stick-to-itiveness; third, common sense." – Thomas A. Edison

A standout and the most essential qualities for all of us to develop is the ability to persevere through life's difficulties and obstacles. It is very significant to constantly be aware of that EVERYTHING COUNTS throughout our life. Every single action you take daily either rewards you somehow or harms you. Everything either takes away or adds up. Everything either adds to your prosperity or moves you far from it. Nothing you do is unbiased. And all achievement is, at last, the triumph of perseverance. The Power of perseverance helping you to skips once more from difficulties and inspires you to become unstoppable toward accomplishing your objectives.

Stage 1 to getting into the magic of perseverance is to know where you are today and in addition know where you need to go. At the end of the day, shooting darts in the dark and seeking for the best is equal to living your life without clear objectives. Try not to stress if your objective seems unrealistic. Before the Wright Brothers, it was out of mind to feel that a man could fly in a plane. What's more, before yesterday December 8, 2007, a sophomore has never won a Heisman Trophy. It's safe to say that if you can vision it; want it bad enough; and willing to sacrifice and persist, almost anything is achievable. Step 2 is to make peace and harmony with the fact that you will face one obstruction after another to achieve your objective. Some goals are short-term and can be accomplished in a while or in a year. Other objectives might take a lifetime to accomplish. In either case, you will continue to face hurdles and you need to prepare yourself to meet them head-on with self-belief. You need to ACCEPT that they'll be there. How could it be another way? No person is all-knowing, so misfortunes and setbacks are BUILT INTO our life's path.

Stage 3 is to persevere and defeat every obstruction en route UNTIL you achieve your objective. The energy and drive to persevere under the harsh situations is the thing that separates the individuals who make it to the end goal. At the point when obstacles show up...you must PERSIST. When you don't know which approach to turn...get help and PERSIST. And most importantly, if you ever think that you're defeated find an approach to continue onward and PERSIST. Furthermore, Help and assistance for the most perseverant people wonderfully seem to appear from some of the most unexpected individuals and places at the opportune time. Persevering people simply appear to figure out how to step forward and prop up when circumstances become difficult. The history books are loaded with these motivating stories.

Obstructions are tough. They knock you down. But they are not intended to KEEP you down. They are intended to revitalize your will, your boldness, your confidence, and your energy. Anyone can succeed and do well staying strong with the breeze at their backs. But what about when the when the wind is at your face and you end up ON your back? As Tiger Woods said in regards to the terrible days, "you have to find it within yourself to get it done." Researchers have discovered that individuals that define obvious objectives for themselves, and decline to stop, will bounce back from any from any misfortunes and accomplish MOST of their objectives. At the end of the day, you can accomplish any objective you set for yourself as long as you fight till your last trail, and decline to allow the inevitable difficulties and frustrations to dissuade you from your course.

Find the Power of perseverance

Here are suggestions for achievement in any field, and some other objective you strive for everyday life:

- Be determined.
- Be stubborn!
- Do not take no for an answer.
- Be single-minded.
- Learn from your mistakes—widen your horizons.
- Don't limit yourself. You may need to take a major move to get the start you need.
- Seek out every single chance.
- Read as much as possible.
- Never think you aren't good enough.
- Develop a set of connections and leverage it.

- Seek out new experiences and environments, and chiefly anyone with a wealth of experience.
- Collect a few qualifications (a degree, maybe an industry certificate) but then make it a priority to collect contacts and experiences, too.

Take time right now to assess your own circumstances and determine your next point of convergence for increasing your perseverance in financial matters. Whatever your big, recent accomplishment, select a new one slightly larger and requiring a longer time commitment. Then lay out your plan and get started. Plan now to keep repeating this process, congratulating yourself occasionally for your growing ability for perseverant work, until consistent work on all your goals is naturally kept up with ease. In this way, you will experience the power of perseverance for yourself.

How to Develop the Power of perseverance?

Majority of people are great at setting goals, but not at attaining them. Whether it is for mastering an instrument or starting up a new business- we love to start things without concluding. One of the major reasons why we never attain our objectives is due to a lack of willpower, perseverance, and motivation. We start out with loads of optimism about the journey, without fully being mentally geared up for the inevitable obstructions ahead. As Tony Robbins states, "success in anything is 80% psychology and 20% mechanics." Perseverance is the difference between failed and successful outcomes? In such a case, it behooves us to build up the excellence of perseverance. When hurdles arrive, perseverance can help you move around, over, or through them. The purpose of perseverance to any task is often what sets apart successful populace. Spending time each day working towards your objective, for instance, increases your odds of success. It is very critical also to ignore your detractors and keep going when you are faced with breakdown or hardship. Being determined means putting one foot in front of the other, no matter whatsoever would be the situations.

perseverance is probably the most admirable and splendid trait a person can possess. It is the ability to be strong-minded to do or attain something regardless of any setbacks. No great achievement is possible without perseverant work. – As quoted by Bertrand Russell. The distinguishing traits of those who succeed in life against those who don't is due to perseverance. Many have the capacity to set plans and visions toward success, yet only a few accomplish something, because only some sticks to work on their objectives and plans until it is accomplished. Most of them stop before they even initiate or they quit in the middle of their journey. Oftentimes, the reason to quit is anxiety, hardships, and uncertainty. They let their doubts and fears paralyze them from moving with determination toward their goals. Or possibly, their enthusiasm isn't firm enough to drive them to work on it. The most interesting thing about a postage stamp is the perseverance with which it sticks to its job – Napoleon Hill. Developing perseverance is a master skill to success. It is easy to relax and do nothing, or simply live in our comfort zone, rather than face the insecurity and discomfort of sailing thru our objectives. Plus, the idea of failure and adversity is unbearable. However, if you want to create change in your life and attain success, now is the time to develop and master perseverance and determination.

Tips on developing perseverance or perseverance

- **Dream bigger than yourself**

Without a bigger purpose and dream that is greater than yourself, you will quit at the initial stages of complexity, as you will inevitably be knocked down. But when you are attaining something amazing for a significant purpose outside of yourself, the pressure of responsibility alone will push you further than a reason that is self-centered. For instance, if you are learning initially to play the guitar in order to boost your confidence you are much more likely to persevere because it is your keen interest, another example- if you are learning Spanish in order to have a better connection with your life partner, you are much more likely to persevere because your relationship is on the line. Or if you are trying to drop excess weight, think about how joyful, confident, and pleased you will feel, and how that will affect the loved ones around you. Shifting from a self-centered objective to a broad purpose that affects those you love helps you concentrate on what you will get out of it, instead of how tough it is.

- **Make your mind up what you want to achieve and set objectives.**

We all know how setting goals is important to achieve success in any attempt, hence get some time to discover what it is you truly craving. Do you want to get some technical degree, lose 5-10 pounds, run a marathon or be a successful business tycoon? In a study done in New York more than a few years ago, unexpectedly found that people who set short and snappy goals succeeded 90-95% in accomplishing them on time! Interestingly, the one caution was that they only attain their goals if they refused to quit and continued to pull through hardships. To be sure, no major feat has ever been accomplished without the trials and tribulations that go along with it. In the most popular poem Don't Quit Edgar Albert Guest explains and clarifies us plenty of motivation and encouragement to forge ahead, principally when the going gets tough.

- **Prepare for Hardship and Difficulties.**

Be prepared and accept that there will be hurdles and setbacks; then prepare for them. Nothing can be ever accomplished without setbacks, adversity, and hurdles in life to contend with along the way. Henry Ford went bankrupt thrice before he manages to design his first vehicle. However, he afterward succeeded to turn into one of the richest personalities in the Globe. He said: "Failure is merely an opportunity to more intelligently begin again." One such example is about

Thomas Edison. He tried 10,000 times to create the light bulb before he succeeded. His attitude was like "I have not failed. I've just found 10,000 means that don't work." Perseverance is certainly the disparity between successful and failed results due to giving up.

One of the significant methods you can prepare for hardships is to anticipate troubles and have a contingency plan. For instance, if you are trying to drop extra weight, you must know that there will be time and moment when it is not possible to stick to your extra fat burning regimen. In such cases, you must prepare alternative meals ahead of time or be mentally prepared to deviate from your fat loss regimen. Unfortunately, in spite of being prepared in such conditions, there are the majority of people give up totally declaring it impossible to stick any diet. In doing so, they sabotage all healthy eating and give up in an unhealthy one. Another common example would be endeavoring to become a marathon runner and you fail on your first effort at finishing a marathon. Should you quit and never try again? No, not at all! You have to make out where you may have miscalculated your potency level, the type of foodstuff you ate and working out models. After doing some research to find out how to improve, you would then give it another whirl! Moreover bear in mind that when we are overwhelmed with a trouble or intricacy, we don't have time then to develop the determination obligatory to deal with the particular obstruction or set back. But if you can plan in advance for life's ups and downs, we will be psychologically ready when sudden setbacks come upon us.

- **Stay Positive**

The road to victory is not easy, in fact, it's much more challenging, and this is why only a few succeed. There will be innumerable times you will be faced with failures and defeat that if you are weak, you will be succumbing to depressing thoughts of doubts and worries. In order to build up perseverance and sooner or later succeed in your endeavor, always maintain a positive mental attitude, despite circumstances. Keep your thoughts and pay attention to taking action towards your objectives. Avoid negative feelings and thoughts for it will ruin your perseverance and concentration.

- **Should have partners**

As the famous saying goes, "If you want to go fast, go alone. If you want to go far, go together." The great performers in the globe all have supportive partners or team to keep them aggravated and perseverant, from employees, assistants, personal coaches, accountability partners, mentors, —the list goes on. Prominently, we should surround our self with persons who have already accomplished what they want to achieve. Not only will this affect your willpower and speed of learning, but research has shown that it will impact your resiliency and perseverance when things get tough. When you have a clearly-defined objective, with a state of certainty that you can attain it, you influence a system in your body referred as the reticular activating system (RAS), that helps our brains make a decision what information to focus on and what to erase.

- **Avoid Things That Will Take Your Moral Down**

We hear a lot of people talking about resisting temptations and building willpower– that all speak to the habit of procrastination, which will take you away from your objectives. Your approach should be to avoid, rather than resist. You have to avoid anything that will distract you once you have your mind set on achieving something. For example, you take great pride in eating healthy foods. Thus, rather than resist temptation in our kitchen, you must avoid having it there. It is the same when it comes to your work. Avoid things which will take your attention away from your objectives.

- **Teach Others**

Have you ever taught something to someone, and found it simpler to remember? This is because when we teach someone, your brain is able to register the information more efficiently than simply reading about it. As study revealed, it turns out that people retain 90% of things when they teach someone else/use at once, 75% of things when they practice what they learned, 50% of things when engaged in a group discussion, 30% of things they learn when they see a demonstration and 20% of things they learn from audio-visual. This research finding is particularly relevant for those wanting to master a newer skill. If you want to improve your communication skills, do not just watch others do it; you have to immediately use what you have learned. If you are learning a new language, instead of using one-sided interactions like mobile apps or audio tapes, work with a conversation exchange partner or language teacher or to practice what you are learning. The key to learning with perseverance is to use it. "Perseverance is not a long race; it is many short races one after another." – Walter Elliott

- **Develop winning habits**

You want to start your day on the positive note – you can attain by celebrating great habits and your discipline the moment you get out of bed. The moment you open your eyes, get up with a smile. Make up your mind with the positive feel. Exercise. Eat a healthy breakfast. Write in your Gratitude Journal. Read motivating books. Starting your day off this way sets you up for success and you will persevere at whatever dream you have set. Determination and perseverance is a daily habit. "Decide carefully, exactly what you want in life, then work like mad to make sure you get it!" – Hector Crawford

- **Focus on Mastery**

If there is any secret to your success, it has been to concentrate on what you can do fine and work towards mastery level. You can get better and better at jobs that help you to attract confidence, to charge what you are worth, to get the best engagements, to attract the best team. You persist when it comes to reaching the next level of brilliance. This all starts with the very little things – with your workouts, with your pre-planning, with your commitment on a daily basis.

- **Be calm when you have a setbacks**

It is all about progress, not perfection- Developing perseverance takes time and it takes dedication. No one is perfect and satisfied. We all have setbacks. And not everything will happen perfectly in your business either. When you face a setback, get back up and get back in the game. Recognize that this is all part of the life journey. Get up – brush yourself off – and recommit to your objectives. perseverance, *Patience, and Perspiration make an unbeatable combination for success. – As stated by Napoleon Hill.* As those two little creatures show up over the next few weeks – You take charge and come to a decision whether or not it will be the devil or the angel that gets through to you. You decide what objectives you want to attain and to what degree you will persist. It is all possible and it is in your hands.

"We can do anything we want to do if we stick to it long enough." – Helen Keller. Studies have shown that when you are too rigid and paying attention on being determined, you are likely going to become anxious and stressed out. Everything will become a task full of strict processes that you are unable to veer from, and you will neglect your relationships, health, wealth, and everything in your life because of that. Hence, you need to have an easy going attitude to become more determined, perseverant, and maintain a healthy attitude in the process. "I am not judged by the number of times I fail, but by the number of times I succeed: and the number of times I succeed is in direct proportion to the number of times I fail and keep trying." – Tom Hopkins

How perseverance Empowers You?

Have you ever been to a food court and had your favorite food come to the table either the wrong one or unexpected presentation delivered and then had the manager or server rush to cover up the situation (even though it was not their complete mistake). The majority of people nowadays are spending more time training themselves on how to "empower" themselves and follow perseverance in their life. But what does empowerment really mean? In the corporate world, it is all about sharing degrees of power with the lower-level workforce to better serve the customer. It is also about giving workers the permission to give customers a priority and to use their imaginative talents to find solutions when a problem erupts, without having to run to senior management and ask for permission to do something. perseverance empowers us and fostering us to the environment of trust and allows us to learn from successes especially by analyzing failures. Working to create the positive surroundings that empower us has been shown to not only increase satisfaction levels but also improve our morale. It takes practice, training, and the ability to accept mistakes as a part of the learning practice – but it is well worth the attempt in the long run!

Self-determination and perseverance are more than self-advocacy. For few among us it might be as easy as representing choices and preferences, and for others, as complicated as determining future careers. Determination has been also described as "The ability to achieve goals based on the basis of knowing and valuing oneself. Some of the major gears of perseverance and determination are:

- goal setting
- personal management
- knowledge of self and others
- self-advocacy
- effective communication
- decision-making
- problem-solving

The most common goal for us is to enjoy the highest possible quality of life. Therefore, we need to offer the instruction, experiences and encouragement that will allow us to become as self-determined and perseverant. People who are self- determined with determination cause things to happen in their lives. We need to follow some instruction in self-determination and perseverance at all functioning levels. This means, we:

- begin early with choice-making and hands-on experiences
- train and re-train from different techniques
- incorporate this instruction into everyday activities

The perseverance and self-determination skills must be learned over the course of a lifetime. They must be integrated into the variety of everyday activities and must be refined over time. Becoming perseverant and determined is not a short-term procedure that can be packed into a few years. It is the task that is never complete; the task that we should work on our whole lives. Being empowered is to realize that your empowerment exists within you.

perseverance empowers you through these components:

- The sense of self-respect
- The right to have access to prospects
- The right to have and find out choices
- The right to have the power to manage your own life
- The ability to go outside yourself to influence change in the socio-economic environment in which you live.

Being perseverant goes just beyond having control over your own destiny and life; it encompasses a number of interdependent and interrelated factors. Every time you allow somebody or something outside of yourself to give you with happiness, love, or success, you are handing your power over to them. When that happiness, love, or success, isn't made real in your life, they have defeated and dis-empowered you. On the contrary, when you decide to be a loving, caring, self-empowered person, the happiness and success that you desire will begin to attract the very people, events and milestones that strengthen your empowered and perseverant life. When you appreciate and understand that you can control what happens to you and to your life, you have taken the major step to perseverance, self-determination, and power of your life and the route you choose to set for yourself. Regardless of your present or your past, you are in control of your upcoming future. And that future just got here. By learning to follow the power of perseverance and empower yourself you learn to bring balance into your life. You will take pleasure of your life where you are in harmony and peace with yourself and those around you. Now take a deep breath: once you started taking hold of the reins of your life and become a self-empowered and perseverant person, you will gain a new clarity for what is truly significant in your life and what is just so much pabulum that you can discard. That clarity will allow you to make important decisions which are in accord with where you want your life to go. Simultaneously, you will be more cognizant of your undertakings on others and will be more of enrichment to their lives. When you understand the true value of yourself, you grow and life will be deeper and more meaningful.

When you begin to foster a healthier, determined, more self-empowered image, confident of yourself and your attainments, actions, and thoughts–you will...

- Know your sense of worth and you will begin to think about, prepare and plan your life for everything you envision on your life's journey.

- You are bind to take the bold steps needed to awaken yourself to the self-empowered and perseverant person that is there inside you, step forward and take complete control of your destiny and get pleasure from your life!

People develop self-reliance when they are given the space to solve their issues and make mistakes in the procedure. Because you have embraced your self-empowerment, perseverance, and all that encompasses, you won't be so scared to move out of your comfy zone and try something new. Personal empowerment is about looking at who you are and becoming more alert of yourself as a unique person. Personal empowerment includes developing the strength and confidence to set practical and realistic goals and fulfill your potential. Everyone has weaknesses and strengths and an array of skills that are used in daily situations, but all too often people remain unaware of, or underrate their true talents. The individual aiming for empowerment is able to take control of their life by making positive selections and setting objectives. Developing self-consciousness, an understanding of your weaknesses and strengths and following the power of perseverance - knowing your own limitations is the key to personal empowerment. Taking steps to set and attain goals - both long and short-term and developing new skills, acts to increase self-confidence which, in itself, is necessary to self-empowerment and perseverance life. The 'Personal Empowerment' and 'Personal Development' are two areas recommended to stay perseverant.

What is Personal Empowerment?

Building personal empowerment entails reflecting on our personal skills, goals, and values and being prepared to adjust our behavior to attain our objectives. Personal empowerment also means being conscious and aware that other people have their own set of objectives and values which may differ to ours. These generally centre on the idea that personal empowerment gives the person the ability to:

- Take control of their situations and attain their own objectives in their personal and working life.

- Grab opportunities to improve personal growth, performance, and a sense of fulfillment.
- Become aware of their weaknesses and strengths and better equipped to deal with troubles and attain goals.
- Improve the contribution they make both as a person and as a member of a team.

Developing personal empowerment usually incorporates making some fundamental changes in life, which is not always easy. The degree of change required will differ from individual to individual, depending on the person starting point.

Dimensions of Personal Empowerment

The following 'dimensions of personal empowerment' are based on the principle that the greater the range of coping responses the persons develops, the higher their chance to copy effectively with different life situations.

These dimensions are Self Awareness, Skills, Values, Knowledge, and Objectives.

- **Self-Awareness-** It involves understanding the person's character and how we are likely to respond to difficult situations, which enables us to build on our positive traits and be aware of any negative qualities which may reduce our effectiveness. Self-aware public makes conscious decisions to boost their lives whenever likely, learning from past experiences.

- **Skills-** The person's skills are the key resource which enables them to accomplish their desired goals. Skills can be gained through practice, experience, training, and education. It is only by building such skills that person values can be translated into action.

- **Values-** Values are beliefs or opinions that are significant to us but of which we aren't always aware. They can be any sort of perceived obligation or belief, anything we desire and for any reason. The reasons we may prefer one thing over another, or choose one course of action over another, may not for all time be obvious or known; there may be no obvious reason for our values. Nonetheless, our values are significant to us as individuals. In order to be self-aware, it is obligatory to be aware of our values, to perilously examine them and to accept that our values may be distinct from those of others.

- **Knowledge** - Knowledge is essential in the development of skills and self-awareness. Knowing where to find suitable information is in itself a crucial skill. Without information, the choices open to people are restricted, both in their working and personal lives. The internet has provided the simplest way to access huge amounts of information very easily and faster. The problem is then centered on the quality of the information found, and the skill set is apprehensive with finding reliable and precise information.

- **Objectives**- Setting objectives are a means by which a person can take charge of their life. The process of setting an objective involves people thinking about their direction and the values that they would like their lives to follow. Goals should always be both realistic and precise. Choices are made through reflection followed by accomplishment. Setting personal goals gives us a direction in life, this direction is necessary for personal empowerment.

Nobody is born feeling self-empowered. Self-confidence is always learned. Everybody has worries and insecurities. No one feels perfect but some of us magnify our flaws more than others. You can easily empower yourself, following step by step, with tolerance, patience, and determination. It can you're your focus but you can start now to inch your way to become self-empowered and break any People Pleasing Habits you might have! Just Change your Perception and Start Developing Confidence! Confidence acts as the great motivators or the powerful limitations to anybody trying to change their performance and become more empowered. There are majority of people who only undertake tasks that they feel competent enough to perform and it takes extra effort to overcome a lack of self-belief and self-confidence in one's capacities. Self-empowerment involves people continuously challenging their own attitude and what they are able of undertaking.

We all have some of the opportunities to discover and develop new skills. In order to become more empowered, we can aim to:

- Develop confidence and self-esteem.
- Develop trust.
- Understand our weaknesses, limits, and

strengths.

- Developing belief

What is Personal Development?

Personal Development is a method for people to assess their qualities and skills, consider their aims in life and set objectives to realize and make the best use of their potential.

Once you understand your requirements, you will understand your undertakings, and if you understand your actions, you will realize your habits. A significant part of personal development is to get rid of any negative traits and habits. To do that, it is significant to understand:

- why you are keeping it
- why you formed it

Personal Development can be a lengthy and difficult process. For Personal Development you may choose to:

- Be honest: When other people place

their trust in you, do your best to give positive results.

- Share and Co-operate: Share knowledge and resources with others to help them to attain their objectives. Work together toward mutual objectives.

- Be Open: In the sharing of ideas, thoughts, and information. When appropriate also sharing feelings, emotions, and reactions. Plus, try to aim to reciprocate appropriately, when someone shares their thoughts, emotions, or feelings with you.

- Be Accepting: Hold the views and values of others in high respect and regard.

- Be Supportive: Support others when required but also recognize their strengths - allowing them to work towards objectives without your intervention.

Personal development and growth allow you to

be completely positive and practical. Rather than wait for better things to happen, you get your brain into gear and make them happen. You may not always attain your goal, but you will experience the more pleasing life when you commit to pursuing your own goals. Making that pledge to personal development is the first step on the medium to personal fulfillment. Personal development provides you with both the incentive and the way to become the best possible version of you. Ironic as it seems, personal growth and development expand our frame of reference to comprise the people around us instead of becoming more self-absorbed. As the world around expands, so does our alertness of the opportunities and possibilities around us. This possibility state of mind fills us with an attitude of eagerness as we start every new day. Your life is now – made up of a sequence of moments. Live purposely in the present moment and you will start to begin to experience the delight and happiness you seek.

Make Connections

Try to broaden your connections and met some amazing persons through your affiliations. Having them to bounce thoughts off of, get support from, ask questions to, and find out about opportunities from has been astounding for your personal development as well as growth. Connection! Make your name known. Put yourself out there! You never know who may be able to assist you down the line. Having personal and business contact that will help you becomes a better person.

Keep Learning

Don't ever discontinue pursuing knowledge! The more you know the better informed you'll be in future. You can stay abreast of world problems and have confidence when people defy you in conversation. Taking the initiative to teach yourself something new the influential things you can do. Read a new book on a subject you liking most, browse news sites on the internet, join a workout club!

Be Independent

Set up your life and your goals so that you don't have to be dependent on others to get by. Whether this simply means being able to offer yourselves with the basic essentials (clothing, food, shelter, and water) or being positive on your own in social situations, fulfilling these requirements on your own gives you the confidence you need to feel in control of your life. Yet being independent is more than being COMFORTABLE with yourself. You have to be confident enough that you are strong enough to face any circumstances on your own. When you are secure in your abilities and don't rely on a family member or partner to make you feel secure and stable, you are able to increase your self-confidence and get to know yourself better.

Where do beliefs come from – are they truly and completely yours?

Nobody is born with beliefs. Self-belief is acquired from a young age and through our experience in our life. How you were treated and the things you were told when young, become the way you reflect about yourself and the world, and ultimately become your beliefs, whether defeating or empowering. The great thing is this does not mean that our viewpoint is actually true. Just because somebody told us we can't do something or be somebody doesn't mean we have to consider them. Stop defending disappointing beliefs! It's tough, but asks yourself: What do I believe about the world? What do I believe about myself? What do I believe about my prospect? After you have discovered what you believe, it's time to decide what you want to throw out and what you want to keep. What beliefs do I want to modify? What do I want to start believing about my future and myself? You can easily decide what you want to believe. Just kick-out those self-defeating beliefs for a successful and empowering self-image.

Change your perception and change your life

Whatever we believe about, we will move toward this. If you feel good about something, you will move toward it, and if you feel bad about something, move away from it. This is essential because what you think and feel about now, will decide where you go in the future. In other sense, if you believe you will never crack an interview, make a deal, get that new job, have a great relationship, you won't. Your self-beliefs may stick you in a cycle of helplessness, where you never see constructive results. You might have given so many interviews but nothing works out. Self-talk determines your self-concept and self-image, which in turn accumulates to decide your believe. If you change what you belief, you can determine what happens to you. How are beliefs playing a crucial role in your life? Following ways:

- You build your self-image with your own opinion. Be careful what you think.

- Your self-image reacts on how you act. To attain more, alter your opinion of yourself

- You think in three distinct dimensions: words or language, which trigger values,

> which in turn cause emotions.

- Your subconscious accepts what you tell it. You must manage your self-talk

What is your insight of your capacities? How do you act when you are not faking it, when you let yourself flow freely with no conscious control? This is the where you desire to be in your everyday life, in touch with your real self and no limitations on your potential.

What is the insight of your capacities? How do you act when you are not faking it when you let yourself flow freely with no conscious control? This is where you desire to be in your everyday life, in touch with your real self and no limitations on your potential.

People self-regulate at their belief level and will stay put unless they allow themselves to break free. This is why it is so significant to make gradual steps every single day to expand and do something that assists you to improve your perseverant power and break away from limiting beliefs. Taking action can kill the self-limiting fear that may be holding you on reverse gear. Be prepared for the rise in stress as you step out of your comfort zone though. This stress comes from our subconscious mind, which wants us to not to take any risk. This is what makes you feel like you need to go back to "where you belong," or why it's too dangerous to try anything new. Try to pay no attention to this. You can elevate your comfort zone by raising your self-concept and boost the power of perseverance through affirmations and visualization, as well as achieving small objectives along the way. You can also kick start changing your behavior by gratifying desired changes with self-affirming statements, like, "Yes, I'm good at that" or "That's like me".

Setting goals and keep focus to increase energy and creativity

To feel self-empowered and improve willpower it takes a structured process of setting objectives, affirming the change we want in our professional or personal life, and seeing progress along the way. In other words you need to be deliberate and intentional in setting objectives and affirming them. You must believe you can attain what you wish or craving or. Therefore, setting goals is a part of human nature. Goals release energy and creativity from your creative subconscious, and the larger the objective, the greater the energy, drive, and imagination. You can start thinking big at anytime, but it can come naturally as you set and attain goals and increase your energy. Use this energy additionally to start setting big goals.

"Don't allow your situation to become your world." – Bishop T.D. Jakes from Oprah's Life Class. We all have our own story. At times it explains why we can't do anything and other times our story pushes us forward. We might have heard cases where people have a similar story — like lack of income or knowledge— and one person eventually starts gaining success in business while the other is out of work and depressed.

"Does your story empower you or dis-empower

you?" – Tony Robbins. We all have stories in different phases of our life. The facts are always available but you have to think positive and be consistent. The only thing that changes is how we understand them and how we come to a decision to embellish them.

perseverance- Enlighten you to the Path of Success

We live in a society that makes it increasingly simple to justify failures and abdicate responsibility. Too often the news trumpets the reasons why some of the groups do not get what they wish for, and they showcase how those in authority are accountable for others' shortcomings. Whereas there are definitely injustices in globe nowadays, successful persons do not allow them to affect how hard they work or what steps they take for growth and development. Competent leaders keep doing the perfect things for their audiences. They persist through hardships, and in the process, they create a culture of perseverance.

If you start doing research on the key to

success, you will surely discover plentiful resources. Some people will call them the only secrets to success you require to know, while others will refer to this information as factors, elements, steps, principles, or else. However, the actual fact is there's only one thing you cannot go without if you want to achieve something in any area of life, and that is tough work. There is more behind that, though. We are talking about being consistent and focused. That means saying no to hurdles and interruptions for a long time, not wanting fast outcomes but being patient and truly believing in the progressing process, changing your strategies and approach and trying newer things while sticking to your initial vision and always bearing it in your mind.

Success does not happen by chance and it does not happen overnight either. It usually takes strategic activities in a suitable direction to get there. There are so many hardships and failures during the journey than the majority of people allow themselves to admit, it is simply that stories about overnight success sound perfect. At the end of the day, it is completely all about how hard you have worked on the right thing – the one which will get you closer to your objective. But to be eager to spend your valuable energy time, and focus, you will need to truly understand exactly why hard work really matters. Every successful person we have ever met has told their path to success was filled with obstacles and surprises they never thought about before they begin. Things happened they never expected. They experienced both positive surprises and unsatisfactory hardships and setbacks. However, the only thing they all have in common is this: they never gave up!

- **Successful leaders are determined and perseverant**; they perseverantly pursue their objectives. For instance- in a most recent post about business ups and downs, Michael Hyatt makes an in-depth comparison of professionals to amateurs in baseball. perseverance always matters.

- **Successful personalities are not so smarter than you.** They probably do not have secrets; instead, they are just determined. They stay at it and eventually see the best results.

- **Successful personalities reach the high end because they just keep going.** perseverant and determined leaders are also learners. They know they need to update themselves and so they keep learning. One of the famous personalities Stephen Key lists believes learning as one of best tips things that pay off. He stated, "Reading advice from successful people, whether it's online or in a book, can jumpstart your enthusiasm."Motivation, energy, and enthusiasm keep us going.

- **They are always busy, respects their time-** Successful personalities are always busy and therefore it is simply difficult to reach them for the things that you want. As you are mainly interested in asking for their precious time to give you insights into personal endeavors and challenges. Do not expect a speedy return to your emails or phone calls. Remember, it is merely an opportunity for you to test your skills of determination and perseverance. Keep sending the emails and you will be surprised how many successful people are grateful for your drive and find the time to meet with you.

- **You make your own fortune with it-** Average people spend enormous time waiting for things to happen. They make innumerable excuses to postpone taking step, and are distracted all the time. On the flip side, people with objectives, constantly do something incredible and try new stuff to move forward. This way, they are truly creating opportunities. There is one universal law that the more you are paying attention on something and take action connected to it, the more doors you open and the more life offers you chances to get close to your vision. Grabbing new prospects and making the most of them is part of working hard. In addition to this it's the real face of luck.

- **Teaches you values-** You learn to persist, to find ways to be grateful for all you have but still aim higher, to be tolerant, to take action instead of waiting for things to happen, take responsibility and to stop blaming for anything you have or don't have in your life instead. Strenuous work gives you a purpose, it assists you overcome procrastination, laziness, your worries, insecurities, fear of failure, and your bad habits.

Success comes to those who are determined and perseverant

It is our mission to continue living every single day of our life journey striving for greatness and working to become perseverant. On the way, we will find those roadblocks where we feel low and the times in our lives where you want to give up. Want to quit. It is in those moments that greatness is being crafted. You can easily have a look on the Google, study and understand success comes to those who were perseverant and those who do not quit and those who do not falter. "Energy and perseverance conquer every single thing." Remember to always carry on seeking the path and the wisdom that is waiting to be shared by others in the world. As you pass through the dream of life understand there are numerous questions you will have. Know today that there will be thousands of people that hold the response you seek.

Some folks are born with an extraordinary talent and some with a silver spoon with status and money in life. Let's be clear. Those "few people" are without a doubt guaranteed some aspect of 'simple' or 'simpler' in their lives. However, those 'some people' have no life assurance as they aren't guaranteed greatness or are they guaranteed to move down into ruined status. The only real guarantees in Life are internal driven but not external driven; the engine that makes Life go is merely you. And speaking of the 'you engine', while perseverance is a nice thought and is the key.

<1>   If you participate you have a possibility of uplifting no matter what you have to offer.

<2>   If you perseverantly involve yourself, you will elevate above the mass.

You not only have to participate externally but you also have to be active, with some perseverance, within yourself. You have to start the engine and keep it well oiled and engage the gears well, you will get the metaphor. Whatever ability & mental, physical or intellectual resources you have accessible to you don't run on their own. You have to be dynamically nurturing. You have to be patiently honing your talents. It means 'good' deteriorates without nurturing and, maybe worse, never even has a chance to blossom without the involvement and active participation. Old belief states that talent is not eternal. It naturally shrinks. Actively participate with no matter what you got and you can improve upon capacity with perseverance and determination and you can elevate it to some unexpected place so that when at some point you want to calm down it starts slipping downwards to a place where others exist in. No participation and everything, even your ability and skills, just atrophy.

perseverance breeds success and achievement, if you are willing to attain something and better your life then you must strengthen your power of perseverance and willpower. Each person's perseverance has a perseverant streak inside of them. The problem is that this streak is not as powerful as you had expected for. If you find that your perseverance diminishes quite rapidly there is hope for you! It is so simple to talk about wanting success and to lead a healthier and successful lifestyle. It's easy to complain about all the things that you do not have in your life. Instead of argumentative why not put your effort and energy into getting all of those things you so craving? The first step in improving your perseverance is to actually starting thinking with a positive frame of mind. Each time you start to think in a negative manner or set up to say the words 'I can't do that', stop and believe for a moment. What exactly is it that you cannot do? Or is it just that you do not wish to do the task?

Most of the times, it is later that is the most common reason. When you find yourself thinking in a similar way simply question yourself why. Is the job at hand actually too tough or are you exhausted and just has had enough of it? When you can triumph over this way of thinking you will be more than halfway to becoming a determined person. While it is fine to take a gap from a task you should never completely give up. Every so often taking a break is all that is wanted. Once you have had the time to re-energize you are prepared to embark upon the job again. A determined person is some who does not give up and when the going gets hard-hitting they look for ways to handle the circumstances. As you complete any job or achieve a target you will feel proud of yourself. This boost in your confidence will help make you a successful individual. For this reason, you want to lay down small goals or break down bigger projects into smaller segments. This way every part is attainable and will help keep you motivated. This applies to countless different types of situations including working on a repair at home, learning a new instrument, learning a new skill, or dealing with an unpredicted event. The next time you feel like giving up, do not attempt instead think of the way you will feel when the task is finished and then shoot for the moon and persevere until the job is finished.

Hard work and dedication always beats talent every single time. It doesn't matter what your abilities are and how you are performing.

Which could have been nothing but an excuse? The outcomes you generate are what you are graded upon. You should possess the willpower and strength of mind to continue moving forward when you are under continuous pressure. This is what makes a handful of people successful and the majority of them mediocre. Successful people know how to go up to the occasion when their best performance is required the most. You have to work dedicatedly just like Michael Jordan. At any time the game was on the line was exactly when he put on his best performances because he possessed a strong determination to win. You must do the same when it comes to your dealing by remaining determined and focused on achieving your objectives. Building a successful business is a bit like climbing a peak of the mountain: it's an uphill battle most of the way, but the view from the top is pretty impressive. Perseverance and dedication is a significant part of attaining a summit, and it's also essential to creating your success as an entrepreneur. If you doubt the significance of perseverance, ask yourself what kinds of objectives people dream of. Do they yearn for the ones that are effortless to achieve or the ones that are hard work but offer enormous payouts?

If you have an awe-inspiring desire to climb your own mountain and attain your entrepreneurial or any sort of dreams, here are some basic rules to help you value and master the art of perseverance.

1. **If you do not persist in your vision, somebody else will-** The unkind reality is that the planet is full of "could've been" -- populace who have magnificent ideas and goals, but did not have the desire, stamina, yearning, or know how to make it happen. Most of them gave up too quickly because it seemed too hard, too discouraging or too frightening. Simply put, they were not mentally prepared to do what it takes to achieve something. The bleak truth is if you aren't willing to

see your dream through, somebody else probably is and somebody else will thrive and succeed where you gave up. Thus, if you are tempted to ditch your entrepreneurial goals, or if you are inclined to tell yourself that "it should be simpler than this," ask yourself the following queries: Do you want to be someone who let your dream go or the one strong-minded enough to see it through? Do you want to be the one who wonders what could have been if you had merely tried or the one who gave your all and either failed or succeeded? So many success stories are hard won. Those who make it are the individuals who are willing to embrace the challenge.

2. **Use naysayers to your benefit-** Visionaries are at the forefront of their time because they push restrictions and introduce change. To turn into

successful, they must hold true to their vision and keep pursuing it even in the face of hardship and struggle. But persisting in your dream does not mean you should pay no attention to the naysayers. You should not discount all the negative input you get, for the reason that there is value in looking at things from a fresh opinion or standpoint. In fact, it is to your benefit to surrounding yourself with the populace who may not always get your dream, and who will ask thoughtful questions that help you scrutinize and define your strategies and goals. The trick is to discover people who will be objective enough to give you a balanced standpoint and help you hone your dream. Even the best ideas may call for some reshaping and tweaking with the intention to be ultimately successful. The bottom line is that we need to be flexible enough to integrate change as required, but confident enough in your vision to keep going after it.

3. **Be in it for the long haul-** Consistency and stability fuels perseverance. Showing up, day in and day out is the significant thing you can do to set yourself on a path to achieving your dreams and becoming the best entrepreneur you can be. If you slack off for phases of time or seem not committed to your own business, you are basically showing the globe that you are giving up. If you lose your enthusiasm and willpower, what incentive do those around you have for buying into your success? Constancy and stability are how you establish your reputation and show people what you are about through your dealings and not just your words. It is how you get your message out there, and how persons

come to believe in you and your vision. It instills accountability and reveals that you are able to deliver the goods on your promises. When you are in it for the long haul and are constantly without fail moving forward on your stated objectives, you begin to build a community around you based on respect, belief, and faith.

4. **Embrace your imagination (without freaking people out)** - A company that gives emphasis to creative input also fosters creativity and has better chances for distraction and long-term success. If you want to succeed as an industrialist, you must embrace your thoughts and creativity. Creative thinking means opening different ways, embracing different viewpoints and investigating different ideas. It also means going beyond a monotonous approach and constantly considering how to adjust or

branch out. But most of all, creativity is bred through perseverance and willpower. Those aha moments, where the sky seems to open up and you can put forth to pluck the ideal solution to a problem, don't happen in a void. They happen through perseverance and pushing yourself ahead. But be aware that there can be a thin line between being the out-of-the-box thinker, an imaginative, and being a creepy, annoying oddball who seems lost in his or her own world. If you want to achieve something, and get others to buy into your vision, it helps to stumble upon as both ingenious and unbiased. Be aware of how others perceive you.

5. **Nurture those "no" for an answer** – We have all run into hardcore salespeople who merely won't take no relationship. perseverant and successful folks are determined to get you to positive

answers, no matter what. On the flip side, those folks are resolute in their dreams. But they are restricted, failing to recognize that there are situations when they may need to accept a short-term no to nurture a long-standing yes. It is significant to not to take 'negative answer' personally. As there are diverse reasons why our thoughts may be rejected. The New study states that around 75-80 % of prospects decline a proposal four times before sooner or later saying yes. Often a negative reply merely means "not right now" or "I need to be influenced." From time to time people just need time to process and think about it. Shifting a negative response into an affirmative answer often requires you to construct trust through reliability and consistency. You can do this by spending extra time asking questions and listening to the replies and less time trying to impress. Perseverance isn't about ramming your sale pitch down other people's throats. Work on being a better communicator. In reality listen to others' participation, hear their concerns and give kind feedback. Be both consistent and persuasive, and you will receive people's confidence and their sales.

Being perseverant is almost as significant as being consistent and determined. Every OPPORTUNITY that you will follow, if it is good, will perpetually draw OPPOSITION. Keep in mind about the eagle eye in a storm? It "mounts" the winds, like somebody climbing a staircase: look forward to the opposition, and learn to mount it, to take you even high, in the chase of your objectives. Perseverance is a sign of a strong character and inner strength. Without it, you could not make any growth and depart progression. It is the ability that makes one a winner against all odds. It is the individual who keeps going that victories.

Success could be simply so close, and a little more effort time and are mandatory. There is a great feeling of accomplishment when you persevere and don't give up! When you persevere, you catch the positivity and go the whole way, and do not turn back after some steps. Only those that keep going reach their ultimate goal. You have to be determined. It doesn't matter how many times, you hurt and you are turned down. Don't stop merely because you failed; try again, and again, and again! If you are pushing yourself to get a dream job, don't quit because you got a negative response. If you are trying to kick-start your career, don't give up because some guy at work shouted at you! If you begin something, you must be perseverant, and gritty to finish it. And you must be perseverant and Consistent.

ABOUT THE AUTHOR

Positive Thinking Mentor Author Gautam Sharma(gautamsharma.contact@gmail.com)- an intelligent, accomplished, capable, creative professional was born in India, has lived in Asia, Europe, Africa and now living in USA embodies and edifies positive thinking, power of optimism and is sharing insights into human behavior and human potential through philosophical, psychological perspectives with the view of sharing mankind's centuries-old wisdom plus proven, research findings so as to empower people worldwide. The author plans to utilize his strengths of professionalism, wide, varied experiences, creativity and communications' skills to publish the Empowerment Series on improvement, self-help topics. Thank you valued readers for your continuous support, contributions and your favorable feedback. Wishing everybody abundance of positive thinking and better living through the power of optimism.

OTHER BOOKS BY THE AUTHOR

https://www.amazon.com/POSITIVE-THINKING-OPTIMISM-Original-English-ebook/dp/B01HRY684S/ref=asap_bc?ie=UTF8

also

https://www.amazon.com/SELF-CONFIDENCE-ESTEEM-HAPPINESS-SUCCESS-ebook/dp/B076VM1MNR/ref=tmm_kin_swatch_0?_encoding=UTF8&qid=&sr=

and

https://www.amazon.com/JOY-forHEALTHY-HAPPY-LIVING-Empowerment-ebook/dp/B078L6Y1YM/ref=sr_1_5?s=digital-text&ie=UTF8&qid=1515281796&sr=1-5

Discover your full potential: The Universe within

Gautam Sharma

(Dedicated to valued readers, especially those who write positive reviews)

www.ingramcontent.com/pod-product-compliance
Lightning Source LLC
Chambersburg PA
CBHW061804250726
48657CB00001B/270